S0-BSZ-583

Gloriously
GLUTEN FREE

hamlyn

Gloriously
GLUTEN FREE

Fresh & simple
gluten-free recipes
for healthy eating
every day

SUSANNA
BOOTH

Contents

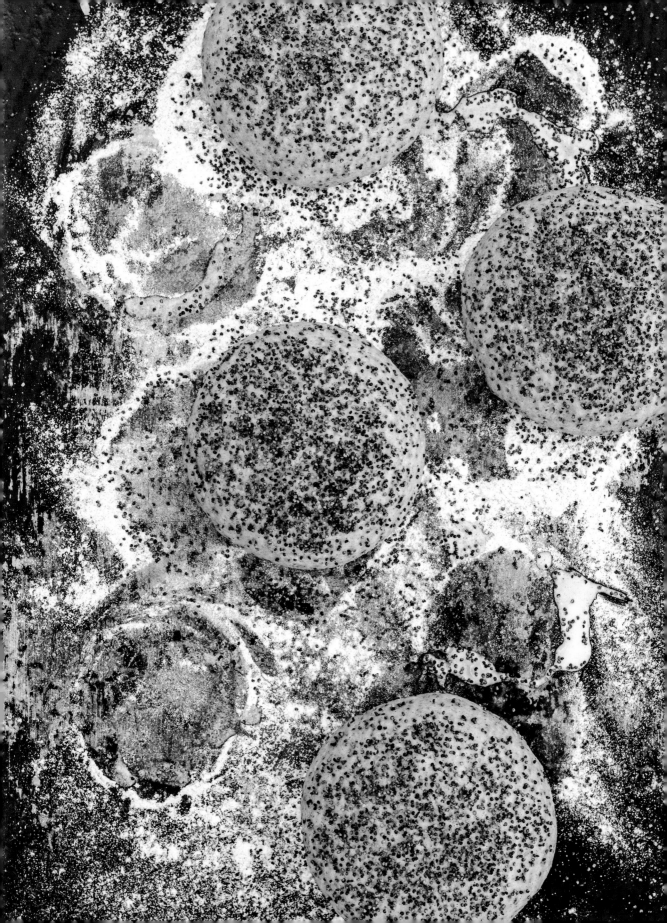

Introduction

Gluten-free lifestyles are increasingly popular, but trying to make gluten-free alternatives to the recipes you love can be a challenge. This is because gluten is a rather special molecule—it is the gluten that makes wheat-based cooking so diverse, from flaky pastries to airy muffins or crunchy, chewy pizzas.

However, if you've so far been dispirited by dense, gritty gluten-free foods, then this is the book you have been waiting for. I have used my science background to take an inventive new look at cooking without gluten. This collection of recipes ranges from the simple to the seductive, but in each case I have chosen the cooking method that will produce the finest possible results: dishes that will delight anyone, regardless of whether they can eat gluten or not. And if you need recipes to suit other requirements as well (like dairy-free, egg-free, nut-free, or vegan), just turn to my Recipe Finder on pages 12–13.

Because gluten-free flours behave differently to wheat flours, merely replacing wheat flour with gluten-free flour in recipes rarely yields the expected outcome. In fact, I found the best results came from thinking about my cooking in a very logical and scientific way. This means some of the methods will be different to those you are used to. For instance, my precooking technique allows you to make (among other things) delicate crepes, a self-saucing hot chocolate pudding, and soft vanilla sponge. My new technique for yeast cooking produces moreish cinnamon spiral buns, thin-crust pizza, and seeded buckwheat rolls. Meanwhile, a simple yet delicious and robust pastry is used in anything from dainty glazed fruit tartlets and pumpkin pie to broccoli and bacon quiche. Gluten-free cooking has to use different methods to get the best results—I'm delighted to share them with you in the pages of this book.

Susanna Booth

Information about Gluten-Free Diets

WHAT IS GLUTEN?

Gluten is a complex protein found in wheat, bulgur wheat, couscous, durum wheat, einkorn, emmer, farro, khorasan wheat (Kamut®), semolina, spelt, and triticale. Barley and rye contain related proteins, while oats are also to be avoided because they are so commonly contaminated during growing and/or processing (gluten-free oats are available, but consult a dietitian before including oats in your diet because they can cause problems for some individuals).

A gluten-free diet can be beneficial for many reasons. Up to 1 in 100 people is estimated to suffer from celiac disease, a permanent autoimmune condition that causes the body to react when it senses even the tiniest amount of gluten, resulting in painful inflammation and damage to the lining of the small intestine. Complete abstinence from gluten is the only effective treatment for this condition. A small number of people are allergic to wheat, barley, or rye. In this instance, the sufferer's body releases a chemical called histamine that can lead to a range of symptoms ranging from itchy eyes, rashes, or sneezing to anaphylactic shock in severe cases. Or you may be among those people who are sensitive or intolerant to gluten, finding that you simply feel better when you don't eat foods containing it.

If you are choosing to go completely gluten-free, it is important to consult your healthcare provider and/or a qualified dietitian before you eliminate gluten from your diet. Wheat flour, especially wholewheat wheat flour, contains fiber, B vitamins, and calcium. Wheat-based products may also be fortified with vitamins and minerals, like iron. It is important to consider this and to plan your meals carefully—the recipes in this book are not intended to form a balanced diet in themselves.

CHOOSING INGREDIENTS

Many ingredients are naturally gluten-free. However, as a rule of thumb, you should avoid all baked goods (such as bread, cookies, cakes, pastries, communion wafers, and matzos), chips, fries, pasta, pizza, stocks, soups, sauces (including soy sauce), and spices unless you know for sure they are gluten-free. You'll need to seek out specifically gluten-free versions of some products or check packaging to make sure the product doesn't contain gluten (some brands of baking powder, mustard, or ketchup contain added flour, for example, but others don't).

The above list of foods to avoid or check is only a guideline—always check the label for gluten-containing ingredients. In some cases, even naturally gluten-free foods are processed or packed in factories handling wheat and this can lead to trace gluten contamination —a problem for anyone who is highly sensitive. Contact the manufacturer if you're unsure.

There is no one product that will act as a direct replacement for wheat flour in every recipe. Gluten-free flours such as buckwheat flour, rice flour, or gram flour all have their strengths and weaknesses. I tend to use brown rice flour because it is reasonably neutrally flavored, has a similar level of carbohydrate to white wheat flour, and contains various trace minerals and vitamins. However, rice flour doesn't absorb liquid as quickly as wheat flour so your dishes will often get a better texture if you leave the batter or dough to rest for 15 minutes or so.

Gluten-free flour blends are good for recipes that require a very neutral flavor (for instance, certain cakes and desserts). You can buy ready-prepared gluten-free flour blends that have been carefully formulated to mimic wheat flour as far as possible. I have based the recipes in this book on my own blend, but by all means use a commercial blend where a blend is required (it doesn't need to have added xanthan gum). If you would prefer to make your own, my recipe is on page 164. You may wonder why I use three different starches (tapioca flour, cornstarch, and potato flour) in my flour blend. The fact is that starch molecules from different sources behave in rather different ways and a mixture is often best.

AVOIDING CONTAMINATION

If you need to be truly gluten-free, then you will also need to ensure every item you use is scrupulously clean. If you have high gluten sensitivity and share your cooking equipment with others, don't use wooden utensils and cutting boards because the cracks may harbor gluten traces. Consider buying kitchen equipment for your exclusive use because it can be very difficult to clean certain items well enough to remove all traces of gluten. These are things such as (and this is not a complete list): toasters, waffle irons, sandwich toasters/panini presses, deep-fat fryers, strainers, wire racks, cake pans, pie weights, and pastry brushes.

Bear in mind that butter, spreads, jams, honey, chutneys, mayonnaise, and dips may also become contaminated by crumbs if shared with others.

INVALUABLE KITCHEN EQUIPMENT

Food processor: If you're eating a gluten-free diet, you'll almost certainly be doing a lot of cooking from scratch. A food processor will make this task a lot less labor-intensive. What I use most is the blending/grinding capability: it allows you to grind your own flours from nuts, puree soups, and grind vegetables, among other things. If your budget doesn't stretch this far, at the very least I would recommend a handheld blender with a food processor attachment. Buy the most powerful one you can afford.

Digital scales: The greater accuracy of digital scales compared with analog, as well as the fact you can set the display back to zero (and thereby add your ingredients to the bowl as you go along), makes them a real help. Some offer liquid volume measurements as well, though be aware that this doesn't really work for oily or very sugary liquids because their density is different to watery ones.

Electric whisk: If you're not blessed with very muscular arms, then a handheld electric whisk is a must. Whipping cream and whisking egg whites is extraordinarily tiring with a manual whisk! Some handheld blenders come with a whisk attachment as a bonus.

CONVERTING RECIPES

As mentioned before, gluten is a complex protein. Gluten molecules love to link up with one another and when they do you get a stretchy gloop. Pour water into wheat flour and you'll get a somewhat gooey mixture that can be kneaded into an elastic dough. This stretchiness allows the dough to form wafer-thin layers—just think of phyllo pastry, the internal structure of fluffy bread or the laciness of crepes.

However, wheat flour also has limitations and it's precisely because of this gluten content. Sometimes we don't want stretchy textures, for example in cakes or in short pastry crust dough. Some of the most common cooking practices are just a way to prevent gluten molecules meeting other gluten molecules. Creaming butter and sugar, then stirring in the flour means the gluten molecules become coated in fat, minimizing the chances of the gluten linking up and resulting in a lighter cake. Keeping short pastry crust dough cool also minimizes gluten linkage, giving a pleasantly crumbly dough, not a tough one that is liable to shrink. Neither creaming nor keeping your batter cool are necessary in gluten-free baking and, in fact, often you need to do the opposite to maximize the interactions within your dough. This may involve some kind of precooking.

If you want to convert your own recipes, here are my top tips:

1 Take your time. If you just use rice flour or a flour blend as a direct substitute for wheat flour, with the same methods, you are likely to end up with gritty and crumbly bakes. For best results, whisk/blend everything really well, then let your mixture rest for a while. Add the raising agent (baking powder or baking soda) mixed with a couple of teaspoons of water just before you transfer the batter to the oven, or the raising agent will be activated too soon and your cake won't rise properly.

2 *Cut down on fat.* Generally speaking, gluten-free flours don't absorb fats and oils nearly as well as wheat flour does and if you're modifying an existing cake recipe this will mean you'll get an oily base. Reduce the butter/oil quantity by about one-fifth.

3 *Xanthan gum: less is more.* Xanthan gum is an additive that helps mimic some of the elastic qualities of gluten and will help to "stick" your ingredients together. It will also minimize the gritty mouthfeel that can be associated with gluten-free baking. It is extremely useful for certain recipes, such as pastry or some breads. However, if you're not a fan of additives, there are many situations for which there is no need to use it, particularly if you have followed Tip 1, above. When you do use it, bear in mind that above a certain concentration it can make a mixture turn slimy—I often use just ¼ teaspoon per recipe.

Recipe Finder

Please note this is a guideline only; all ingredients should be checked for suitability before use.

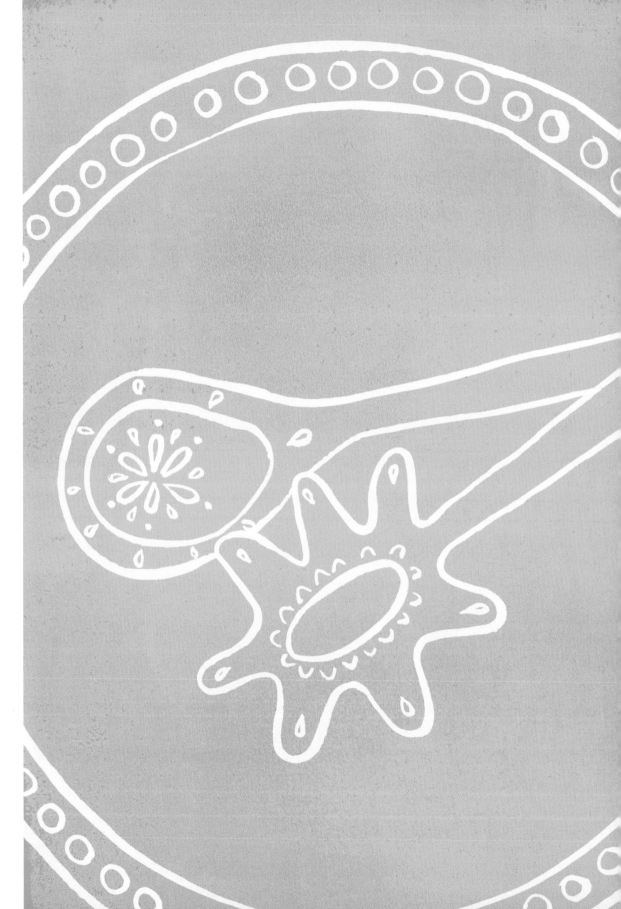

SALADS,
SOUPS
& SNACKS

2 large carrots, peeled and finely grated

4 small dessert apples, cored and coarsely grated

2 tablespoons granulated sugar

2 tablespoons boiling water

juice of 1 lemon

Place the grated carrots and apples in a serving bowl.

Put the sugar and measurement boiling water in a small cup and stir together until the sugar has dissolved. Add the lemon juice and mix together.

Pour the lemon mixture over the grated carrot and apple and stir until well combined. Chill for 30 minutes before serving.

Carrot & Apple Salad

This is a recipe from my mother and probably my favorite salad of all time (I do have a sweet tooth, though). The best part of it is the sweetened lemon dressing, which gives the salad a mouth-filling juiciness. I can eat a mountain of this; it's fantastic and my children beg me to make it, which I can say without understatement is unusual for a vegetable-based dish.

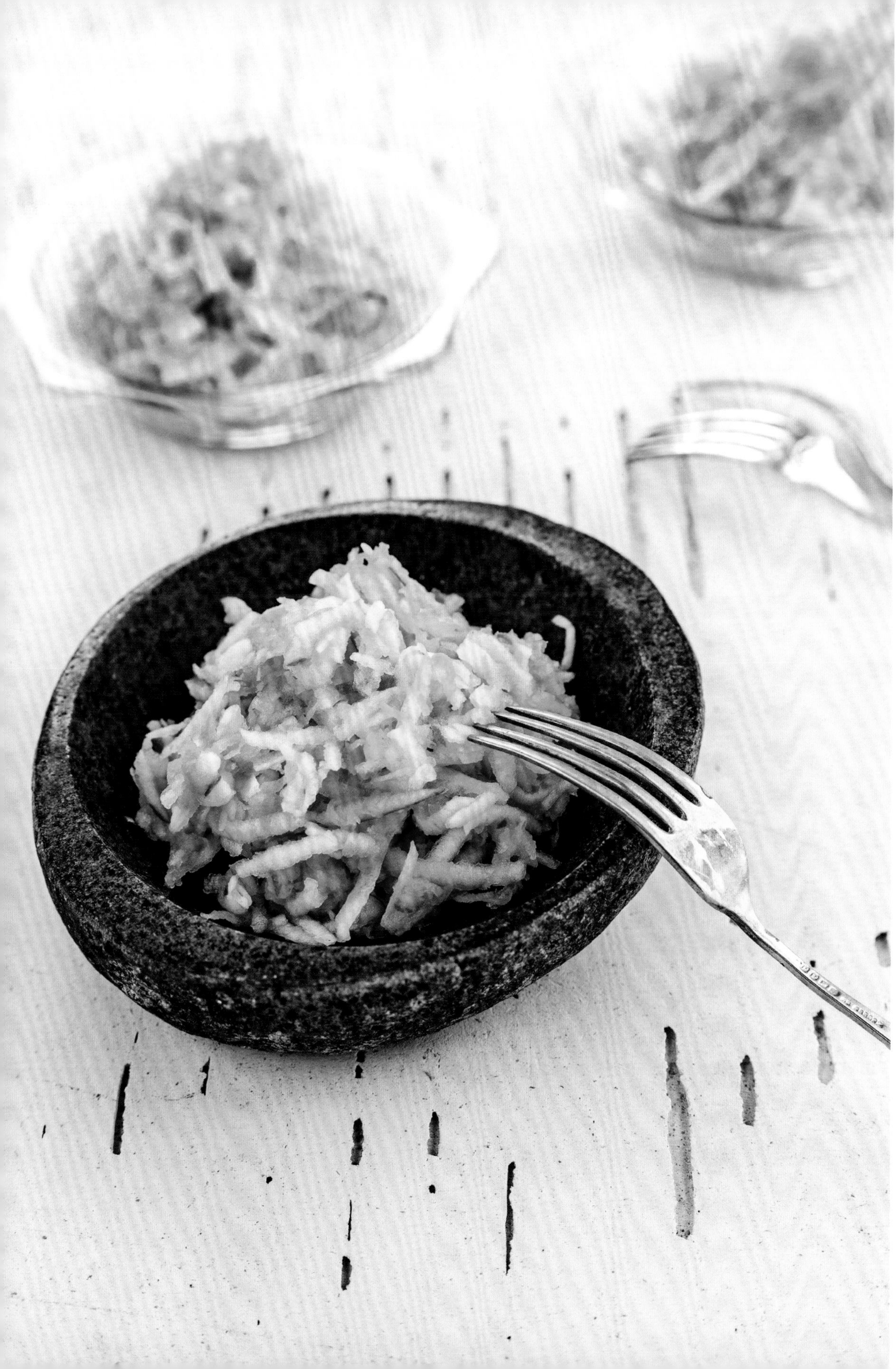

SERVES 3–4

3 small raw beet, about 6oz total weight, peeled, trimmed, and cut into ¼ inch slices

3 large oranges, such as navel

2oz arugula leaves

3½oz seedless grapes, each cut into 3 pieces

1 tablespoon lemon juice

1 tablespoon olive oil

pinch of salt

Cook the beet in a saucepan of boiling water for 10 minutes until tender, then drain and let cool. Cut each slice into quarters and place in a serving bowl.

Using a sharp knife, remove the peel and pith from the oranges, then cut out the segments, remove any seeds, and chop into similar-size pieces to the beet. Add the orange pieces, arugula, and grapes to the beet.

Mix together the lemon juice, olive oil, and salt in a cup, pour over the salad, and toss together. Serve immediately.

Beet & Orange Salad

This is a refreshing yet simple salad with an attractive mix of colors. If you opt for ready-cooked beet, make sure it contains no vinegar, otherwise the flavor balance will be wrong.

1lb mealy potatoes,
peeled and cut into ¼ inch
thick slices

3½ tablespoons unsalted butter

¼ cup cider vinegar

2 teaspoons gluten-free mustard

2 onions, thinly sliced

salt and pepper

Cook the potatoes in a saucepan of boiling water for about 8–10 minutes until they are just starting to disintegrate. Drain, setting aside ¾ cup of the cooking water, then place the potatoes in a serving bowl.

Add the butter, vinegar, and mustard to the reserved water in the pan, return to the heat, and stir until the butter has melted. Add the onions and cook gently until almost soft but a hint of crunch remains—about 2–3 minutes.

Pour the onion mixture over the potatoes and carefully stir together to prevent the potatoes breaking up. Season with a little salt and pepper to taste. Serve immediately.

Warm Danish Potato Salad

This is the perfect salad for serving alongside sausages, especially the frankfurter kind. But it would also work as part of a vegetarian barbecued meal, with corn cobs, griddled mushrooms, and a green salad.

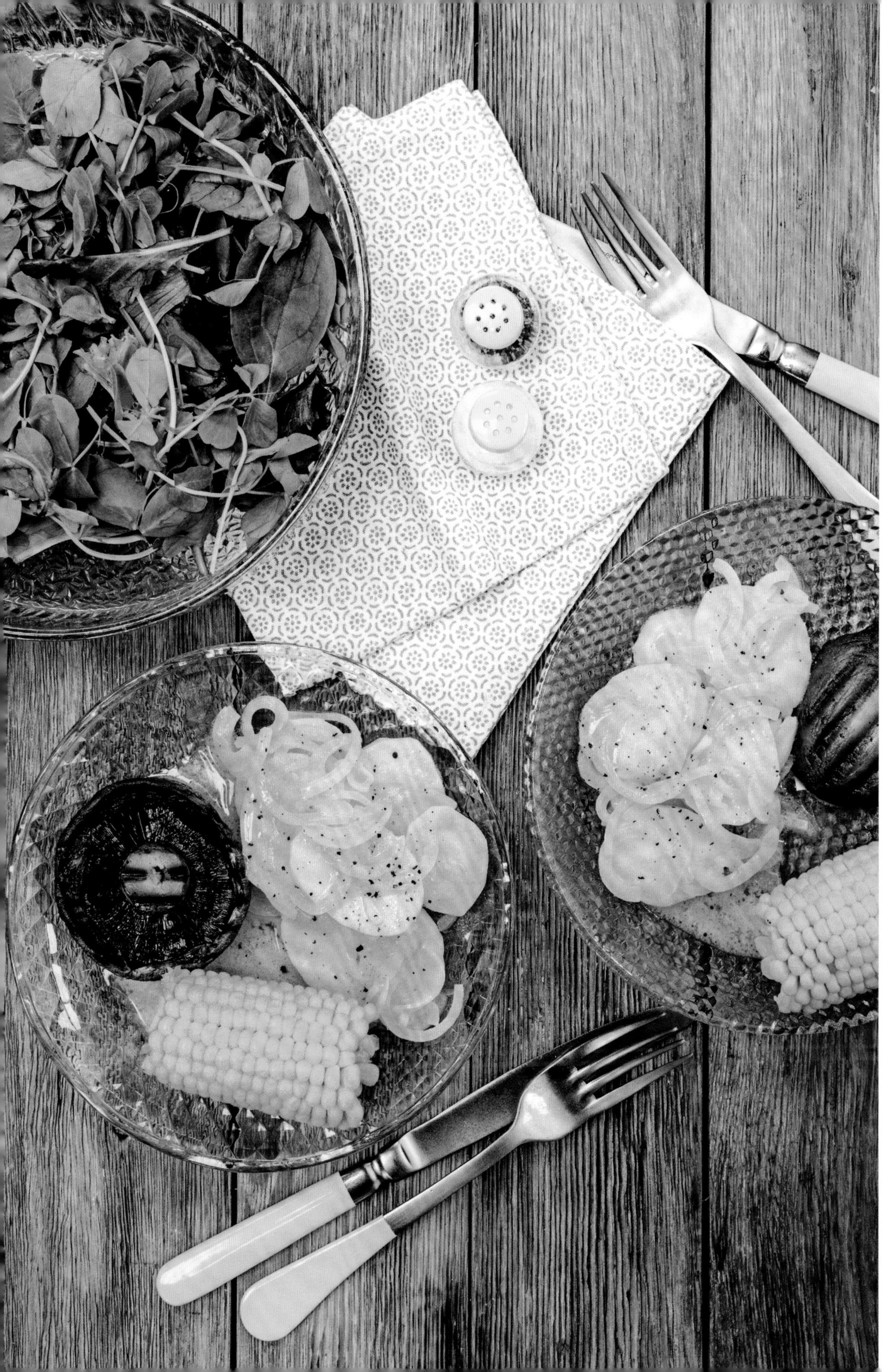

SERVES 4

2 tablespoons olive oil

2 onions, sliced

4 garlic cloves, sliced

2½lb ripe tomatoes, quartered

4 cups gluten-free vegetable stock

10 basil leaves

3 parsley sprigs

4 thyme sprigs

2 thick strips of grapefruit peel

2 tablespoons cornstarch

½ cup light cream

granulated sugar, to taste

salt and pepper

Heat the oil in a large saucepan or ovenproof Dutch oven, add the onions and garlic, and fry gently for about 5 minutes until soft but not brown. Add the tomatoes, stock, herbs, and grapefruit peel and bring to a boil. Reduce the heat and simmer, uncovered, for 30 minutes until the tomatoes are completely soft.

Turn off the heat and let the soup stand for 10 minutes, then press through a strainer to remove the seeds and skin. Pour the soup back into the pan.

Mix together the cornstarch and ¼ cup of the soup in a cup until smooth, then whisk into the soup and bring to a boil, whisking continuously. As soon as the soup bubbles, remove the pan from the heat and stir in the cream. Season to taste with salt and pepper, adding a little sugar if necessary, and serve.

Thick Tomato Soup

I'm a big fan of tomato soup from a can, but a few years ago I made my own—and it was fantastic! I particularly enjoy making a large batch of soup from my juicily ripe homegrown tomatoes, still warm from the sun, and freezing it to enjoy later in the year when the weather has turned cold.

2 carrots, peeled and cut into ⅛ inch thick circles

2 celery sticks, cut into ⅛ inch thick circles

2lb chicken wings

2 bay leaves

2 teaspoons salt

½ teaspoon ground black pepper

8½ cups water

1 tablespoon chopped parsley

13oz gluten-free noodles, cut into 2 inch lengths

Place the carrots, celery, chicken, bay leaves, salt, pepper, and measurement water in a large stockpot. Bring to a boil, uncovered, then reduce the heat to medium-low and simmer for 3 hours, skimming off the fat with a spoon if necessary.

Leaving the pan on the heat, transfer the chicken pieces to a bowl using tongs, then remove the bay leaves and discard.

When the chicken is cool enough to handle, remove the skin and break off chunks of the meat. Return the meat to the soup, discarding the skin and bones.

Add the parsley, then bring the soup to a boil. Stir in the noodles and cook according to the package directions until tender. Serve hot.

Chicken Noodle Soup

This is a comforting soup for a cold day—or just because you have a cold! Though standard noodles are not suitable for gluten-free diets, this soup can be made with chopped-up rice vermicelli, gluten-free tagliatelle pasta, or (my favorite) sweet potato vermicelli or cellophane noodles, also known as dang myun.

SERVES 4

4 teaspoons olive oil

4 large leeks, trimmed,
cleaned, and roughly sliced

1lb mealy potatoes,
peeled and roughly chopped

6¼ cups water

4 parsley sprigs

2 thyme sprigs

2 bay leaves

½ cup light cream

salt and pepper

chopped chives, to serve

Heat the oil in a large saucepan or ovenproof Dutch oven, add the leeks, and cook gently until softened but not brown. Add the potatoes, measurement water, herb sprigs, and bay leaves and bring to a boil, then reduce the heat and simmer for about 30 minutes until the potatoes are tender. Remove the pan from the heat and let stand for 15 minutes, then remove the herbs.

Using a handheld blender or a food processor, blend the soup until smooth, then pass through a strainer and season to taste with salt and pepper.

To serve, return the soup to the pan, add the cream, and heat through until almost boiling. Serve sprinkled with chopped chives.

VARIATION
Use soy cream in place of the light cream to make a dairy-free version of this recipe.

Leek & Potato Soup

My most memorable bowl of leek and potato soup was in a French restaurant in Vietnam—the velvety smoothness and delicate flavor were so strikingly different to the local dishes I'd had. It seemed amazing that such variation could exist. The French call this soup vichyssoise and serve it cold, but personally I think it is a lot nicer served hot.

SERVES 4

1 tablespoon olive oil

1 onion, diced

1 leek, trimmed, cleaned, and
cut into ½ inch pieces

2 carrots, peeled and cut into
½ inch pieces

2 celery sticks, cut into
½ inch pieces

3 garlic cloves, finely chopped

2 rosemary sprigs, leaves chopped

handful of basil leaves, chopped

1 (13oz) can borlotti beans
(or other bean of your choice),
rinsed and drained

2 (13oz) cans chopped tomatoes

¼ cup risotto rice or short-grain
pudding rice

4 cups gluten-free vegetable stock

1 white cabbage, halved, core
removed, and leaves roughly
chopped

4 savoy cabbage leaves, tough
stalks removed and roughly
chopped

salt and pepper

Heat the oil in a large saucepan or ovenproof Dutch oven,
add the onion, leek, carrots, celery, and garlic, and stir well
to coat in the oil. Cover with a lid and let cook gently for about
5 minutes.

Add the chopped herbs, beans, tomatoes, rice, and stock,
cover again, and cook for about 20 minutes.

Place the chopped cabbage on the surface of the soup, cover
again, and cook for 5 minutes until just tender, then stir the
leaves into the soup and cook for another 5 minutes. Season
to taste with salt and pepper and serve.

Minestrone

A bowlful of this soup has a kaleidoscope of colors and makes
a great meal in itself. Though minestrone commonly contains
pieces of pasta, here I've opted to use short-grain rice instead.

MAKES 4

1 tablespoon sunflower oil, plus extra for greasing

¼ cup lukewarm water

1 teaspoon active dry yeast

1 teaspoon granulated sugar

½ cup tapioca flour

½ cup milk, plus extra for brushing

1¼ cups buckwheat flour, plus extra for dusting

¼ teaspoon salt

2¼ tablespoons poppy seeds

½ cup sunflower seeds

VARIATION

Use soy milk in place of milk for a dairy-free version of this recipe.

Grease a large baking sheet with sunflower oil.

Stir together the warm water, yeast, and sugar and set aside.

Place the tapioca flour, milk, and oil in a saucepan over medium-high heat and cook, stirring continuously, until it all clumps together in a sticky mass. Remove from the heat.

Place the buckwheat flour and salt in a large bowl. Stir in the yeasty liquid, then add the tapioca mixture. Using a spoon, turn the lump over until it is well coated in the flour. Using your hands, gradually knead in all the remaining flour: hold the lump of dough in both hands with your thumbs uppermost, then move your hands as if you are opening a book—this will gently stretch the top of the dough. Tuck the stretched dough underneath. The freshly exposed dough on top will be sticky, so dunk it in the flour. Repeat the stretching, tucking, and dunking until there is no more loose flour left.

Turn the dough out onto a counter well dusted with flour and continue to knead for another 1 minute until well combined (keep your hands well floured). Setting aside 2 teaspoons of the poppy seeds for sprinkling, knead the remaining seeds and the sunflower seeds into the dough.

Cut the dough into 4 equal-size pieces and shape into round rolls. Place the rolls on the prepared baking sheet. Brush with a little milk and sprinkle over the reserved poppy seeds. Let rise in a warm place for about 1 hour, or until doubled in size.

Preheat the oven to 325°F. Bake for 25 minutes until browned and they sound hollow when you tap them. Let cool for a few minutes before serving.

Seeded Buckwheat Rolls

Deliciously crusty outside and spongy inside, these rolls are mainly made from buckwheat, a naturally gluten-free seed, but the key to success is the tapioca flour. When it is heated with liquid it becomes super-stretchy—perfect for bread.

5oz sweet potatoes, peeled and coarsely grated

2½ cups Gluten-Free Plain White Flour Blend (see page 164)

8oz unsweetened chestnut puree

3 tablespoons soft dark brown sugar

½ cup water

¼ cup sunflower oil

3 eggs

½ teaspoon gluten-free ground nutmeg

pinch of salt

1½ teaspoons gluten-free baking powder

⅔ cup pecans

2 tablespoons flaxseeds

Preheat the oven to 300°F. Line a 2lb loaf pan with nonstick parchment paper.

Place the sweet potatoes, flour blend, chestnut puree, sugar, measurement water, oil, eggs, nutmeg, and salt in a food processor and blend until well mixed. Let stand for 15 minutes (this improves the final texture).

Add the baking powder and pecans to the sweet potato mixture and blend for a few seconds, then stir in the flaxseeds. Pour into the prepared pan and smooth the top with a spatula.

Bake for 60–70 minutes until the edges of the loaf are pulling away from the pan and a skewer inserted in the center comes out clean. Transfer the loaf to a wire rack and let cool.

Chestnut & Pecan Loaf

This moist and nutritious high-fiber loaf is lovely thickly sliced and served with cheese, or spread with butter as an accompaniment to soup. It will keep for a couple of days in an airtight tin.

SERVES 4–6

2 tablespoons olive oil

1 red onion, sliced

2 teaspoons chopped rosemary

½ cup milk

1 teaspoon balsamic vinegar

1 egg

1 tablespoon tomato paste

1⅓ cups cornmeal

½ teaspoon baking soda

½ teaspoon salt

Heat half the oil in an 8 inch nonstick skillet over a stove ring about the same diameter as the pan. Add the onion and rosemary and cook over medium heat for about 2–3 minutes until the onion is slightly translucent.

Meanwhile, put the milk, vinegar, egg, tomato paste, and remaining oil in a small bowl or pitcher and mix together. In a separate bowl, stir together the cornmeal, baking soda, and salt. Quickly pour the wet ingredients into the dry ingredients and stir well, then pour into the skillet, level with a spatuala, and cover with a lid.

Reduce the heat to low and cook for 8–10 minutes. The steam will help to cook the bread and it's done when the center becomes solid – the surface should look dry and a skewer inserted into the center should come out clean. Remove the pan from the heat and keep covered. To serve, invert onto a plate.

VARIATION

Use soy milk in place of the milk to create a dairy-free version of this recipe.

Stovetop Italian Cornbread

This bread is a cross between an American cornbread and an Italian focaccia. It is best eaten warm, and you can easily whip it up just before a meal. Because no oven is needed, this is a brilliant recipe for a camping trip, too.

SERVES 4

2 tablespoons salted butter,
softened, plus extra for greasing

1 cup tapioca flour

¼ cup boiling water

¼ cup olive oil

⅔ cup finely grated Parmesan or
other hard cheese

1 egg, lightly beaten

1 garlic clove, crushed

2 teaspoons chopped parsley

Preheat the oven to 350°F. Lightly grease a baking sheet
with butter.

Place the tapioca flour in a heatproof bowl. Pour over the
measurement boiling water and stir vigorously (there will
still be quite a lot of dry flour, but this is normal). Stir in the
oil and grated cheese, then add the egg and stir thoroughly
to create a sticky dough.

Spoon the dough out onto the prepared baking sheet, then
using a spatula, pat it into a large oval about ½ inch thick.
Bake for 20 minutes until puffed up and browned.

Meanwhile, place the garlic and butter in a bowl and mix together,
then mix in the parsley. Remove the flatbread from the oven
and smear it with the butter. Return to the oven and bake for
another 10 minutes. Serve hot.

Garlic & Parmesan Flatbread

Cheese and a top smothered with garlic butter raises this flatbread
above an everyday offering. Perfect for tearing and sharing,
it's based on Brazil's pão de queijo, but with an Italian twist.

1 tablespoon olive oil

2 onions, thinly sliced

2 eggs

2 teaspoons thyme leaves,
plus extra sprigs to garnish

Dough

5 tablespoons cold unsalted
butter, diced, plus extra for
greasing

1/2 cup plus 2 tablespoons brown
rice flour, plus extra for dusting

3/4 cup gram (chickpea) flour

1/2 teaspoon xanthan gum

4 teaspoons gluten-free
wholegrain mustard

1 tablespoon water

Preheat the oven to 350°F. Grease the sections of a 12-cup tart pan with butter.

To make the dough, place the rice flour, gram flour, and xanthan gum in a bowl. Add the butter and rub in with the fingertips until the mixture resembles bread crumbs. Stir in the mustard, then add the measurement water. Using your hands, combine well to form a soft but not sticky dough, adding a little more water or rice flour if necessary. Wrap in plastic wrap and chill for 30 minutes.

Roll out the dough to about 1/8 inch thick on a counter dusted with rice flour. Stamp out 12 circles using a pastry cutter a little larger than the pan sections. Alternatively, use a jar lid to cut around. Press the dough circles into the pan sections. (Don't worry too much about perfection, but if there are cracks or holes use a little of the excess dough to fix them.) Bake for 10 minutes, then let cool in the pan.

To make the filling, heat the oil in a nonstick skillet, add the onions, and cook over medium heat for about 5–10 minutes until softened and starting to turn brown.

Beat together the eggs in a pitcher, then add the thyme leaves. Stir in the warm onions, then use a fork to transfer the mixture evenly into the pastry shells.

Bake for 10 minutes until the filling has set. Carefully remove the quiches from the pan, then serve warm or cold, garnished with thyme sprigs.

Mini Onion Quiches with Mustard Pastry

A nutritious alternative to wheat flour, gram flour is particularly good in savory dishes. Here the mustard marries well with the sweetness of the onions and earthiness of the thyme. Try these little quiches for a picnic, in a lunchbox, or as a party snack.

2 onions

1 tablespoon olive oil, plus extra for greasing

¾ cup gram (chickpea) flour

½ teaspoon gluten-free ground turmeric

¼ teaspoon gluten-free ground coriander

¼ teaspoon gluten-free ground cumin

pinch of salt

2 tablespoons water

1 tablespoon mango chutney

1 teaspoon tomato paste

Preheat the oven to 350°F.

Cut the onions in half, top to bottom, then slice each half into ⅛–¼ inch slices. Heat the oil in a nonstick skillet, add the onion slices, and fry gently for about 5 minutes until soft but not brown.

Place the gram flour, spices, and salt in a bowl and add the fried onions. Add the measurement water, chutney, and tomato paste and stir together until the mixture is smooth but not sloppy— it should be moist enough to make stirring easy.

Drizzle a lipped baking sheet with oil, then place 8 dollops of the onion mixture onto the sheet using tablespoons. You might need to flatten the heaps a little with the back of a spoon.

Bake for 15 minutes, then remove the sheet from the oven and gently move it from side to side to redistribute the oil. Using a spatula, flip the bhajis over, then return to the oven and bake for another 15 minutes until well browned and glistening.

Onion Bhajis

Onion bhajis are one of my favorite snack foods, but until I tried to make them I didn't realize they could be so easy. I don't have a deep-fat fryer, so this version can be done on a baking sheet in the oven. Eat these the same day, hot or cold, and serve with mango chutney or a dip made of plain or soy yogurt and chopped fresh mint.

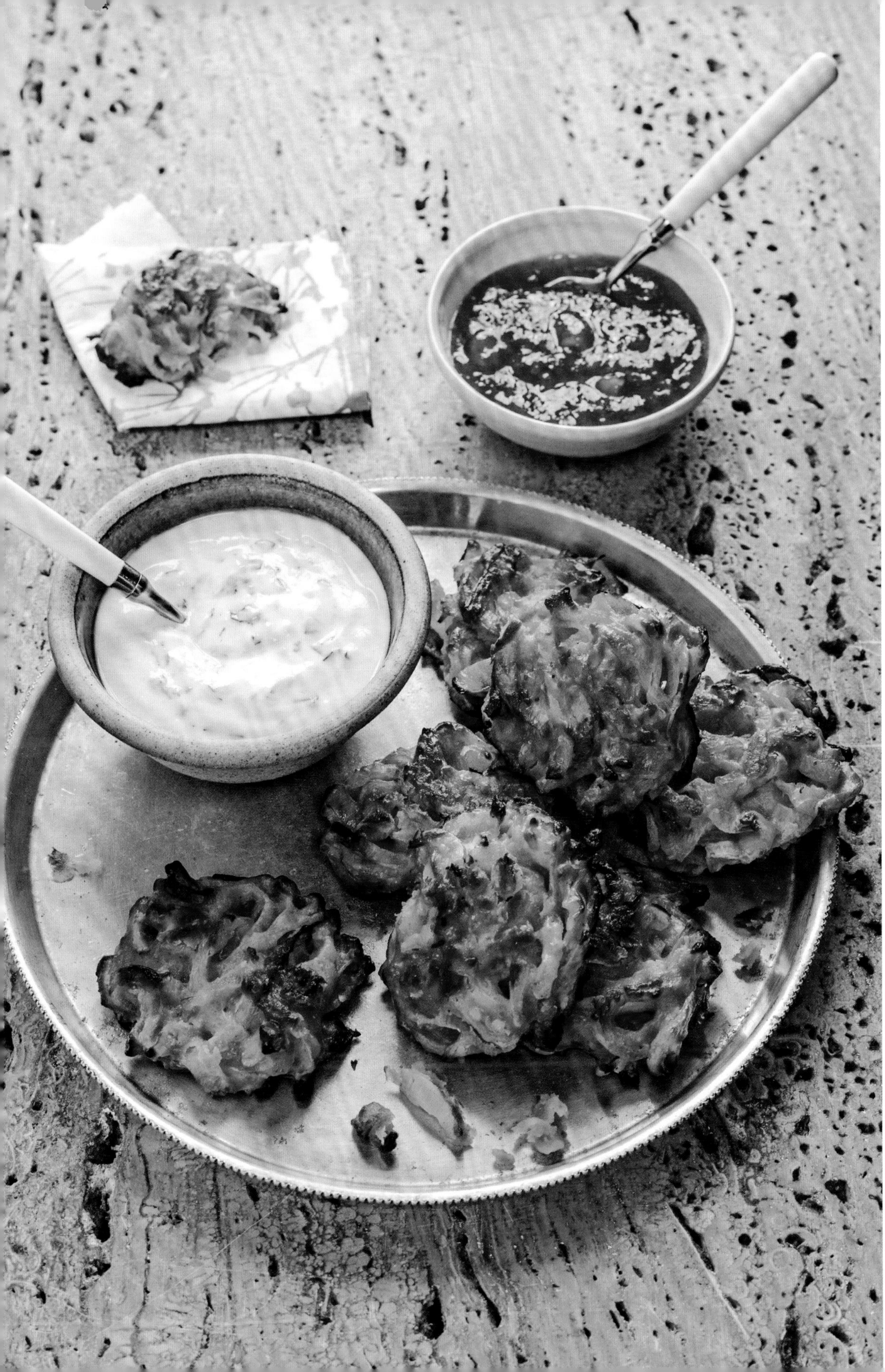

2 teaspoons olive oil

1 small onion, finely diced

2 teaspoons gluten-free curry powder

2oz peeled potatoes, finely diced

1 small carrot, finely diced

2 teaspoons tomato paste

1 teaspoon mango chutney

½ cup water

¼ cup frozen peas

½ teaspoon salt

1 tablespoon chopped fresh cilantro

sunflower oil, for shallow-frying

Dough

1¼ cups Gluten-Free Plain White Flour Blend (see page 164)

1 cup gram (chickpea) flour, plus extra for dusting

½ cup water

2 tablespoons olive oil

½ teaspoon xanthan gum

1 teaspoon poppy seeds

pinch of salt

To make the dough, place all the ingredients in a bowl and combine to form a soft but not sticky dough, adding a little more water if necessary. Wrap in plastic wrap and place in the refrigerator to chill.

Heat the olive oil in a heavy saucepan, add the onion, and fry gently for about 3–4 minutes until softened. Add the curry powder and cook for another 10 seconds, then stir in the potatoes, carrot, tomato paste, chutney, and measurement water. Cover with a lid, reduce the heat to low, and simmer for 5 minutes until the vegetables are just tender. Add the peas, salt, and cilantro, then remove from the heat and set aside.

To make the samosas, roll out the dough to about ⅛ inch thick on a counter dusted with gram flour. Using a 6 inch diameter bowl or side plate as a template, cut out 6 dough circles, then cut each circle in half. Wet the curved edges with a little water and fold over the semicircles to form rough triangle shapes, pinching the curved edges shut to form cones of dough. Spoon 2 teaspoons of the filling into each dough cone and seal the remaining edges by dabbing with a little water and pinching shut.

Arrange 4 samosas in a circle in a deep skillet or saucepan. Pour in sunflower oil to the depth of about ½ inch and heat over medium-high heat. Fry the samosas for about 1–2 minutes until golden brown, then flip them over using a slotted spoon and fry for another 1–2 minutes. Remove from the pan with a slotted spoon, drain on paper towels, and keep warm in a low oven while you cook the remaining samosas.

Vegetable Samosas

Forget the store-bought flaccid triangles that masquerade as samosas—these homemade ones are delicately crispy and golden brown. Cut the vegetables into tiny chunks, otherwise the samosas will break open. Eat within a couple of days.

2 teaspoons olive oil,
plus extra for greasing

4 teaspoons gluten-free curry
powder

1 quantity gluten-free Plain Short
Pastry dough (see page 166)

3½oz ground lamb

1 small onion, finely chopped

1 garlic clove, finely chopped

½ teaspoon cayenne pepper

¼ teaspoon gluten-free
ground cinnamon

¼ teaspoon gluten-free
ground ginger

¼ teaspoon ground black pepper

¼ teaspoon salt

2 teaspoons tomato paste

¼ cup frozen peas

¼ cup water

cornstarch, for dusting

Preheat the oven to 350°F. Lightly grease a baking
sheet with oil.

Knead half the curry powder into the dough, then wrap
in plastic wrap and chill while you make the filling.

Heat the oil in a saucepan, add the lamb, and fry over
medium heat for about 10 minutes, breaking it up with
a wooden spoon, until browned and cooked through. Drain
off any liquid and transfer the lamb to a bowl. Set aside.

Add the onion and garlic to the pan with the remaining
curry powder, cayenne, cinnamon, ginger, pepper, and salt
and fry gently for about 5 minutes until the onion is softened.
Add the lamb, tomato paste, peas, and measurement water
and cook for another 5 minutes, then remove from the heat.

Roll out the dough to about ¼ inch thick on a counter
dusted with cornstarch (if the dough starts to crack,
knead in a drop of water). Stamp out about 12 circles
using a 3½ inch diameter pastry cutter. Alternatively,
use a jar lid to cut around.

Place 1 heaping teaspoon of the filling on the lower half of
a dough circle, then lightly wet the edge with water. Fold
over the top half of the dough and press the edges together
to seal. Using your fingertip, form a frilled edge (if the
dough starts to crack, brush with a little water). Repeat
with the remaining dough circles and filling.

Place the pasties on the prepared baking sheet and bake
for 25 minutes until golden. Serve warm or cold.

Curried Lamb Pasties

For a time I lived in Brixton, London, where I discovered the
delights of Caribbean cooking. These little pasties are inspired
by traditional Jamaican patties, with their spicy lamb filling and
curried pastry, and are great for lunchboxes, picnics, or parties.

1 cup water

½ cup quinoa, rinsed and drained

¼ cup pine nuts

1lb lean ground lamb

1 small onion

4 teaspoons cornstarch

4 teaspoons red currant jelly

4 teaspoons chopped rosemary

1 teaspoon gluten-free ground cinnamon

1 teaspoon salt

½ teaspoon ground black pepper

olive oil, for drizzling

Preheat the oven to 325°F.

Pour the measurement water into a saucepan and bring to a boil, then add the quinoa and simmer for 15 minutes, or according to the package directions. Remove the pan from the heat and let stand until all the liquid has been absorbed.

Meanwhile, toast the pine nuts in a dry skillet until lightly browned.

Place the lamb, onion, cornstarch, red currant jelly, rosemary, cinnamon, salt, and pepper in a food processor. Add the toasted pine nuts and blend to a thick paste. Stir in the quinoa.

Divide the mixture into 12–15 equal-size balls and form into egg-shaped patties. Place on a baking sheet and drizzle with olive oil. Shake the sheet to coat the kibbeh in the oil.

Bake for 15 minutes, then remove from the oven and gently move the kibbeh around on the sheet. Increase the oven temperature to 350°F and return the kibbeh to the oven for another 15 minutes until nicely browned and cooked through —cut the largest kibbeh in half to check the meat is cooked; if not, cook them a little longer.

Kibbeh

Kibbeh are meat snacks from the Middle East, traditionally made using bulgur wheat, which contains gluten. This simple version uses quinoa instead.

1 cup sushi rice

2¼ cups water

2 teaspoons rice vinegar

½ ripe avocado

1 carrot, peeled

½ yellow bell pepper, cored and seeded

¼ cucumber, seeded

2 sheets of sushi nori (dark seaweed sheets)

Place the rice in a heavy saucepan, add the measurement water, and bring to a boil. Cover with a lid, then cook over medium heat for about 15 minutes until the rice is tender and the liquid has been absorbed. Let cool, then gently mix in the rice vinegar.

When ready to assemble, pit and peel the avocado, then dice into ⅛ inch cubes along with the carrot, yellow bell pepper, and cucumber.

Place your first sheet of sushi nori, shiny side down, on a sushi mat or clean dish towel, aligning it with the bottom edge. Spread half the rice evenly across the sheet, leaving a ½ inch strip at the top uncovered. Lay half the vegetables over the width of the rice, leaving about ¾ inch of rice uncovered at the top and bottom.

Starting at the bottom of the sheet, apply an even, gentle pressure while you roll it up to form a tight sausage of sushi, using the mat or dish towel to help you. Lightly wet the top strip and press to form a seal. Using a sharp knife (it can help to wet the blade a little), cut the roll into 10 slices. Repeat with the remaining ingredients.

Simple Sushi

Though sushi is most commonly associated with fish, there are actually lots of possible vegetable fillings and it is also really easy to make. Don't be put off if you lack a sushi mat because a clean dish towel works just as well. Serve with tiny bowls of gluten-free tamari, wasabi paste, and sushi ginger. Eat the same day.

10oz cooked peeled shrimp, rinsed and drained

⅓ cup brown rice flour

¼ cup water

2 teaspoons chopped chives

1 teaspoon gluten-free ground ginger

4 teaspoons chili oil

pinch of salt

2 egg whites

sunflower oil, for shallow-frying

sweet chili sauce or garlic mayonnaise, to serve

Pat the shrimp dry using paper towels and set aside.

To make the batter, stir together the rice flour, measurement water, chives, ginger, chili oil, and salt in a bowl. In a separate, thoroughly clean bowl, whisk the egg whites until frothy, stopping before they get to the soft-peak stage. Add the rice mixture and whisk until combined. Stir the shrimp into the batter.

Pour sunflower oil into a wok or large saucepan to the depth of about ½ inch and heat to 340°F, or until a drop of batter sizzles gently in the oil.

Using tongs or chopsticks, gently drop about 8 shrimp into the hot oil and fry for about 1 minute until golden, then flip over and cook for another 1–2 minutes until golden-brown all over. (The shrimp should bubble gently with a constant sound of gentle sizzling and without violent spitting.) Remove with a slotted spoon and drain on paper towels. Repeat until all the shrimp are cooked. Serve immediately with sweet chili sauce or garlic mayonnaise.

Shrimp in Spicy Tempura

Tempura batter is a Japanese specialty and making it with rice flour works really well. This recipe uses shrimp, but strips of carrot, zucchini, or red bell pepper are also delicious. Most conventional recipes stress the need for ice-cold water, but that's not necessary for this gluten-free version. Use the batter as soon as it is made.

3½ tablespoons butter

¾ cup cornstarch

1 cup gluten-free vegetable stock

1oz ham, finely diced

¼ teaspoon salt

¼ teaspoon ground black pepper

½ cup instant cornmeal

sunflower oil, for shallow-frying

Melt the butter in a heavy saucepan, then stir in the cornstarch and whisk until lump-free. Gradually add the stock, whisking until smooth. Bring to a boil and cook for about 2 minutes, stirring continuously, until thick. Stir in the ham, salt, and pepper, then let cool completely (the mixture will then be very firm and easy to mold).

Tip the cornmeal into a bowl. Take 1 tablespoon of the ham mixture and shape it into a cylinder about the length of your index finger. Roll it in the cornmeal until well coated, then transfer to a plate. Repeat until all the ham mixture is used up—it makes about 10 croquetas.

Pour sunflower oil into a heavy saucepan to the depth of about ½ inch and heat to 350°F, or until a small cube of gluten-free bread sizzles in the oil. Using a slotted spoon, lower the croquetas into the hot oil and fry for 2 minutes on each side (they won't go brown). Remove with a slotted spoon and drain on crumpled paper towels. Serve hot.

VARIATION
Use scant ¼ cup finely chopped cooked mushrooms in place of the ham for a vegetarian version.

Ham Croquetas

Often served as a tapas dish, ham croquetas, or croquettes, are defined by a creamy interior and crisp exterior. These croquetas are made in the traditional way—with a filling made from Béchamel sauce, rather than potato—while the crunchy coating is simply a layer of cornmeal.

SAVORY

8oz fresh asparagus, trimmed and cut into ¾ inch pieces

1 quantity gluten-free Plain Short Pastry dough (see page 166)

Spinach filling

5oz spinach leaves, tough stalks removed

½ cup ricotta cheese

2 teaspoons garlic puree

1 egg

Hollandaise filling

scant ¼ cup cornstarch, plus extra for dusting

7 tablespoons unsalted butter

⅔ cup ricotta cheese

2 eggs

juice of ½ lemon

¼ teaspoon salt

Preheat the oven to 350°F.

Cook the asparagus in a saucepan of boiling water for about 8 minutes until very tender, then drain.

Meanwhile, roll out the dough to about ¼ inch thick on a counter well dusted with cornstarch. Line an 8 inch tart pan with the dough and trim any excess using a sharp knife.

To make the spinach filling, steam the spinach for about 1 minute until it wilts, then squeeze out any moisture. Blend the spinach, ricotta, garlic puree, and egg in a food processor or blender until smooth.

Scatter the asparagus over the pastry shell, then pour in the spinach mixture.

To make the Hollandaise filling, melt the butter in a saucepan, then stir in the cornstarch and whisk until smooth. Add the ricotta, eggs, lemon juice, and salt and whisk until combined. Spoon the mixture evenly over the spinach in the pastry shell.

Bake for 30 minutes until the filling is set and has started to brown slightly.

Asparagus, Spinach & Hollandaise Tart

Buttery soft asparagus is mixed with spinach in a lemony Hollandaise-style filling, while the combination of dark green and pale yellow make this vegetarian tart particularly attractive. This tart can be enjoyed hot or cold.

SERVES 4–6

8oz cherry tomatoes

2 finger-length rosemary sprigs

2 teaspoons olive oil

1 quantity gluten-free Plain Short Pastry Crust dough (see page 166)

cornstarch, for dusting

½ cup soft goat cheese, such as chèvre blanc, cut into small pieces

3 eggs

¼ cup milk

salt and pepper

Preheat the oven to 250°F.

Wash and dry the tomatoes, then place in a small roasting pan with the leaves from the rosemary and the olive oil. Toss the tomatoes to coat them in the oil, then bake for 30 minutes.

Meanwhile, roll out the dough to about ¼ inch thick on a counter well dusted with cornstarch. Line an 8 inch tart pan with the dough and trim any excess using a sharp knife. Scatter the goat cheese evenly over the pastry shell.

Beat together the eggs, milk, and a little salt and pepper in a small bowl.

Tip the roasted tomatoes, rosemary, and oil into the pastry shell and spread out evenly across the shell. Pour over the egg mixture.

Increase the oven temperature to 350°F and bake the tart for 30 minutes until golden and the filling is set.

Roast Tomato, Rosemary & Goat Cheese Tart

This tart was a favorite of mine after I left university and it has been an easy meal option ever since. I love it with a fresh green salad and boiled new potatoes.

2 teaspoons olive oil

1 small onion, roughly chopped

2 garlic cloves, roughly chopped

1 (13oz) can chopped tomatoes

2 tablespoons tomato paste

¼ teaspoon salt

2¼ cups grated mozzarella cheese

basil leaves, to garnish

Dough

¾ cup tapioca flour

1 cup milk

2½ teaspoons active dry yeast

2 teaspoons granulated sugar

¼ cup lukewarm water

1¾ cups Gluten-Free Plain White Flour Blend (see page 164), plus extra for dusting

2 tablespoons olive oil, plus extra for greasing

1 tablespoon dried milk

½ teaspoon salt

cornmeal, for dusting

To make the dough, place the tapioca flour and milk in a saucepan and heat, stirring occasionally, until it comes together as a very stretchy white lump. Remove the pan from the heat.

Stir together the yeast, sugar, and warm water in a cup. Place 1¼ cups of the flour blend in a large bowl and add the oil, dried milk, and salt. Add the tapioca mixture to the bowl and, using a spoon, turn the lump over until it is well coated in flour.

Pour in the yeasty liquid and knead together until a dough forms, then turn it out onto a counter lightly dusted with flour blend and continue to knead for 1 minute. Put it back in the bowl, cover with oiled plastic wrap, and leave in a warm place for about 1 hour until doubled in size. Knead in the remaining flour blend, then let rise for another 30 minutes.

Meanwhile, heat the oil in a saucepan, add the onion and garlic, and fry gently for about 5 minutes until softened, then add the tomatoes, tomato paste, and salt. Simmer for 4 minutes until the sauce is reduced, then let cool slightly. Using a handheld blender or food processor, blend the sauce until smooth.

Preheat the oven to 350°F. If you have a pizza stone, pop it in the oven; if not, preheat a baking sheet.

Turn the dough out onto a counter dusted with flour blend and cornmeal. Divide the dough into 4 equal-size pieces and shape into thick circles. Place 1 circle on the preheated pizza stone or baking sheet and use your fingers to carefully spread out the dough until it is about ¼ inch thick. Spread a layer of tomato sauce on top and sprinkle with a quarter of the mozzarella. Repeat with the remaining dough to make 4 pizzas.

Bake for 15 minutes until golden and the cheese has melted. Serve immediately, topped with basil leaves.

Pizza Margherita

This recipe will make four cheese and tomato pizzas with light, airy bases—what you choose to add to them is up to you! Cooked tapioca flour gives all-important stretchiness to the dough, while cornmeal adds a touch of authenticity and crunch.

2 onions, roughly chopped

1 red bell pepper, cored, seeded, and roughly chopped

1 green bell pepper, cored, seeded, and roughly chopped

2 zucchini, roughly chopped

8oz cherry tomatoes, halved

3 garlic cloves, thinly sliced

¼ cup olive oil

1 oregano sprig

2 thyme sprigs

1 eggplant, cut into ¾ inch cubes

4 teaspoons tomato paste

salt and pepper

Preheat the oven to 350°F.

Place the onions, bell peppers, zucchini, tomatoes, and garlic in a roasting pan, add the oil, oregano, and thyme and toss together. Roast for 20 minutes until just tender.

Place the eggplant and tomato paste in a large saucepan, scrape in the roasted vegetables, including the oil, and stir well.

Cook over medium heat for 20 minutes until all the vegetables are tender. Season to taste with salt and pepper and serve.

Roast Vegetable Ratatouille

Ratatouille is a jewel-colored Provençal dish that uses tomatoes, eggplant, bell peppers, and zucchini. It is typically cooked on the stovetop, but in this version I start off the process in the oven for a slightly sweeter taste. I like to serve this ratatouille with fish or gluten-free pasta, in particular.

SERVES 4

2 tablespoons unsalted butter,
plus extra for greasing

1 teaspoon olive oil

8oz mushrooms,
finely diced

⅓ cup cornstarch

¾ cup gluten-free vegetable stock

¾ cup grated Gruyère cheese

2 teaspoons gluten-free
wholegrain mustard

3 eggs, separated

Preheat the oven to 350°F. Grease a deep 29oz (3½ cup) ovenproof dish with butter.

Heat the oil in a nonstick skillet, add the mushrooms, and fry gently for about 5 minutes until golden. Set aside.

Melt the butter in a saucepan, then stir in the cornstarch, and whisk until it forms a lump-free paste. Gradually add the vegetable stock, stirring continuously until the sauce is thickened. Remove the pan from the heat and stir in the grated cheese and mustard. Let cool for 10 minutes.

Whisk the egg whites in a thoroughly clean bowl until stiff. Stir the egg yolks and mushrooms into the cheese sauce, then carefully fold in the whites. Pour the mixture into the prepared dish and bake for 45 minutes until puffy and golden brown.

Mushroom & Gruyère Soufflé

This soufflé is great on its own as an appetizer, or served with new potatoes and green vegetables as a main. Don't be put off by any stories you may have heard about soufflés being temperamental: I've been cooking them since I was about 12 years old and have never had a problem. You don't even need to be too worried about the exact cooking time: by turning the heat down to about 225°F you can keep your soufflé quite happy for 10–15 minutes until needed (just don't open the oven door until the last minute or your masterpiece may collapse).

SERVES 4

1 tablespoon olive oil

1 onion, diced

2 leeks, trimmed, cleaned, and finely sliced

2 celery sticks, finely sliced

2 carrots, peeled and cut into ½ inch cubes

2 small parsnips, peeled and cut into ½ inch cubes

2 zucchini, cut into ½ inch cubes

1 red bell pepper, cored, seeded, and sliced

1 yellow bell pepper, cored, seeded, and sliced

5 closed cup mushrooms, sliced

1 (13oz) can gluten-free baked beans

salt

Dumplings

7 tablespoons pure vegetable fat, chilled in the freezer

1⅔ cups gram (chickpea) flour

⅓ cup cornstarch

1 teaspoon gluten-free baking powder

handful of parsley, chopped

pinch of salt

¼ cup water

Heat the oil in a large ovenproof Dutch oven, add the onion, leeks, and celery and cook over medium heat for about 5 minutes until softened. Add the remaining vegetables to the pan and cook for another 5–10 minutes until soft.

Add the baked beans, then half-fill the empty can with water and add to the pan. Cover with a lid and bring to a boil, then reduce the heat and simmer for 1½ hours. Season to taste with salt.

Toward the end of the cooking time, preheat the oven to 325°F. To make the dumplings, grate the frozen vegetable fat into a bowl. Stir in the gram flour, cornstarch, baking powder, parsley, and salt, then add the measurement water and knead to a soft but not sticky dough, adding a little more water if necessary. Divide the dough into 8 equal-size pieces and shape into balls, then drop them into the stew.

Transfer the pan to the oven, uncovered, and cook for a bout 35 minutes until the dumplings have browned on top. Serve immediately.

Vegetable Cobbler

This vegetable stew formed more or less my staple diet at university. I serve it here with dumplings, which bake in the stew while it cooks in the oven, and end up with crispy tops and fluffy middles.

SERVES 4

1lb butternut squash, peeled, seeded, and cut into ½ inch cubes

¼ cup olive oil

4 green cardamoms

2 teaspoons cumin seeds

10 whole cloves

2 onions, finely chopped

4 garlic cloves, finely chopped

thumb-size piece of fresh ginger root, peeled and finely grated

2 teaspoons ground black pepper

4 teaspoons gluten-free curry powder

1 teaspoon granulated sugar

2¼ cups tomato sauce

2 (13oz) cans chickpeas, rinsed and drained

7oz spinach leaves, tough stalks removed and torn into pieces

salt

Preheat the oven to 350°F.

Place the squash in a roasting pan and toss together with half the olive oil until evenly coated. Bake for 45 minutes until golden brown and tender.

Meanwhile, remove the seeds from the cardamom pods and place in a mortar and pestle or spice grinder with the cumin seeds and cloves. Grind to a fine powder.

Heat the remaining oil in a large heavy saucepan over medium-high heat, add the onions, and fry gently for about 5 minutes until softened. Add the garlic, ginger, pepper, curry powder, and ground spices and cook for a few minutes.

Stir in the sugar, sauce, and chickpeas. Fill 1 empty chickpea can with water and add to the pan, then reduce the heat and simmer for 20 minutes. Stir in the cooked squash and simmer for another 10 minutes.

Place the spinach on top of the curry, but don't stir in—leave for a few minutes until the leaves wilt, then stir them in and season to taste with salt. Reduce the heat to medium and cook for another 5 minutes.

Squash & Spinach Curry

This curry is inspired by my favorite in my local bar—it's full of flavor but not too spicy. Real Indian curries tend to use lots of spices, some of which are quite unusual, so I've tried to make it as simple as possible. If you don't already have cumin, cloves, or cardamoms and don't fancy buying them, simply replace them with an extra teaspoon of curry powder (just make sure it's gluten-free). This is delicious served with boiled basmati rice, poppadums, lime pickle, and mango chutney.

3 eggs, separated

½ cup plus 2 tablespoons brown rice flour

¼ cup milk

¼ teaspoon salt

sunflower oil, for shallow-frying

1¾lb sustainably sourced boneless white fish fillets, such as Alaska pollock, cut into large pieces

Whisk the egg whites in a thoroughly clean bowl until they form soft peaks. Using the same whisk, whisk the egg yolks, rice flour, milk, and salt in a separate large bowl until well combined. Fold the whites into the yolk mixture to form a thick batter.

Pour oil into a large saucepan to the depth of about ½ inch and heat over medium-high heat to 340–350°F, or until a drop of batter sizzles gently.

Using a fork, dip 2 or 3 pieces of fish in the batter mix until both sides are coated, then very carefully lower them into the hot oil using the fork or a slotted spoon. Fry for 3–5 minutes on each side until the batter is dark golden and the fish is cooked through. Remove with a slotted spoon, drain on paper towels, and serve while still crispy.

Repeat with the remaining fish and batter, adding more oil if necessary and removing any stray bits of batter with a slotted spoon (or they will start to burn).

VARIATION

You can use water in place of the milk for a dairy-free version of this recipe.

Battered Fish

This tempura-style recipe gives a crunchy coating to fish and doesn't need a deep-fat fryer. Try it served with Simple Tomato Sauce (see page 170) and rice, or with French fries and peas in the classic British way.

6 eggs, separated

2 tablespoons pesto

½ cup brown rice flour

⅔ cup cream cheese

1 tablespoon finely chopped chives

¾ cup whipping cream

1 garlic clove, crushed

4oz smoked salmon, cut into small pieces

2 tablespoons olive oil

Preheat the oven to 350°F. Line a jelly roll pan or roasting pan with nonstick baking paper.

Whisk the egg whites in a thoroughly clean bowl until they form soft peaks. In a separate large bowl, whisk together 1 tablespoon of the pesto and the egg yolks until the mixture has doubled in volume. Sift over the flour and add the whisked whites, then gently fold together.

Pour the mixture into the prepared pan and gently smooth the top with a spatula. Bake for 15–20 minutes until just cooked through. Lay a clean dish towel over the roulade and flip it over. Lift off the pan, then gently peel away the paper. Roll up the roulade and dish towel to form a sausage and let cool.

Meanwhile, mix together the cream cheese, chives, and 2 teaspoons of the cream in a bowl until smooth, then add the garlic. Whip the remaining cream, then add to the garlic mixture and fold together.

When the roulade has cooled, unroll it carefully and spread the cream mixture evenly over the surface, leaving a ¾ inch strip uncovered at one short side. Scatter the salmon over the surface, then gently roll up the roulade, starting at the end that has the filling spread to the edge. Place on a serving plate, seam side down, and trim the ends.

Mix together the remaining pesto and oil in a small bowl, then serve the roulade cut into slices and drizzled with the sauce.

Smoked Salmon & Pesto Roulade

As an elegant main course this roulade is hard to beat. It is served cold, so can be made in advance—even the day before if necessary. The pesto sauce is also lovely drizzled across boiled new potatoes.

3oz gluten-free white bread

5 tablespoons cold unsalted butter, diced

1 small onion, roughly chopped

large handful of dill

grated zest of ½ unwaxed lemon

pinch of salt

1lb piece of boneless salmon fillet, skin on

Preheat the oven to 325°F.

Place the bread in a food processor and pulse to form bread crumbs. Spread out the crumbs in a roasting pan and bake for about 30 minutes, stirring occasionally, until dried out and browned.

Place the crisp crumbs in the food processor with the butter, onion, dill, lemon zest, and salt. Blend for a minute or so until the mixture forms a paste, then shape into a ball.

Increase the oven temperature to 400°F.

Place the bread crumb mixture on a sheet of plastic wrap and, using your hands, flatten into a slab about the same size and shape as the salmon fillet. Cut a piece of aluminum foil about 5 inches wider and longer than the fish and place it in a roasting pan. Place the salmon in the center, skin side down, then carefully lift up the crust on the plastic wrap and flip it onto the fish. Peel off the plastic wrap and pinch the corners of the foil together to form a shallow tray, but don't cover the crust with foil. (This will allow the salmon to steam gently in the buttery juices without drying out, while the crust stays crisp.)

Bake for 25 minutes until the fish is just cooked through and the crust has turned golden brown. Serve immediately.

Salmon with a Dill Crust

This recipe takes a slab of salmon and tops it with a neat crumbed herb crust, a technique I learned from Gordon Ramsay's lovely book, *A Chef for All Seasons*. It looks impressive but is actually very simple—the most time-consuming part of the process is drying out the bread crumbs, for which you'll need to allow half an hour. Serve with steamed slices of zucchini.

1¼lb mealy potatoes, such as Russet, scrubbed (or peeled, if preferred) and cubed

¼ cup olive oil

3½ tablespoons unsalted butter

2 carrots, peeled and finely grated

1 leek, trimmed and finely sliced

2 eggs

11½oz sustainably sourced white fish fillet, such as cod or Alaska pollock, cut into 3 pieces

2¼ cups milk

⅓ cup cornstarch

½ cup grated cheddar cheese

sea salt

Preheat the oven to 350°F.

Cook the potatoes in a large saucepan of boiling water for about 10–15 minutes or until tender, then drain. Roughly mash with the olive oil and set aside.

Meanwhile, melt half the butter in a small saucepan, add the carrots and leek, and fry gently for about 8 minutes until soft, then transfer to a 9 inch square baking dish.

Rinse out the pan, then add the eggs, cover with cold water, and bring to a boil. Cook for about 6–7 minutes until hard-cooked, then cool under cold running water.

While the eggs are cooking, place the fish pieces in another pan, pour in the milk, and poach the fish gently for about 5 minutes until cooked through. Drain the fish, setting aside the cooking liquid, then remove any skin and bones and flake the flesh into the baking dish.

Using the poaching pan, make the sauce. Melt the remaining butter, then stir in the cornstarch and whisk until it forms a lump-free paste. Gradually pour in the reserved milk and the cheese, whisking continuously. Increase the heat and continue to whisk until the sauce thickens. Pour it over the fish.

Shell the eggs and roughly chop, then add to the baking dish and stir until well combined. Spread the mashed potato over the top and sprinkle with sea salt. Bake for 30 minutes until browned and heated through.

Fish Pie

This fish pie elevates a simple piece of white fish into a feast. You'll need three pans, but don't let it put you off because it is well worth the extra cleaning up. I particularly like this pie with a good helping of peas.

SERVES 3–4

2¾ cups gluten-free cornflakes

¼ cup rice flour

2 teaspoons gluten-free vegetable
stock powder

1 egg

2 tablespoons milk

10oz dense sustainably sourced
skinless white fish fillet, such
as Alaska pollock, cut into
3 x 1½ inch fingers

1 tablespoon sunflower oil

Preheat the oven to 325°F.

Place the cornflakes, rice flour, and vegetable stock powder
in a food processor and blitz to a fine powder, then tip onto
a plate. Beat together the egg and milk and pour into
a shallow dish.

Dip each finger of fish first in the egg mixture, then in the
crumbs, turning them over until fully coated. Place on a
baking sheet and drizzle with the oil. Using tongs, move the
fish fingers about, turning them over until both sides are
lightly coated in the oil.

Bake for 15 minutes until the coating is crispy and the fish
is cooked through.

Fish Fingers

This is a very simple way to create a golden crunchy
crumb on fish using cornflakes and a few pantry staples.
Get your fish suppliers to prepare the fish for you—to make
finger shapes, you'll need a piece of fish about ½ inch thick,
with the skin removed.

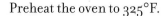

SERVES 4

3½oz gluten-free
white bread

3½ tablespoons unsalted butter,
softened

2 teaspoons garlic puree

2 teaspoons chopped parsley

4 boneless, skinless chicken
breasts, about 7oz each

1 egg

Preheat the oven to 325°F.

Place the bread in a food processor and pulse to form bread crumbs. Spread out the crumbs in a roasting pan and bake for about 30 minutes, stirring occasionally, until dried out and browned.

Meanwhile, make the filling. Place the butter, garlic puree, and parsley in a small bowl and stir together. Shape the mixture into marble-size lumps, then place the bowl in the freezer.

Lay 1 chicken breast on a clean counter. Using a small, sharp knife, make a horizontal cut about 1 inch long in the underside of the breast—aim for the thickest part of the breast, about a third of the way down. Carefully (so you don't puncture any further holes or indeed your own hand) wiggle the knife about to create a pocket as large as possible—try not to enlarge the initial cut while you do this. Alternatively, create the pocket using your finger. Repeat with the remaining chicken breasts.

Insert 3 or 4 lumps of the butter into each pocket. Skewer the cuts shut with toothpicks—if you accidentally make holes elsewhere, skewer those shut as well. Cover and chill the chicken breasts for 15–30 minutes.

Beat the egg on a large plate. Tip the bread crumbs onto another plate. Dip each chicken breast into the egg, then the crumbs, turning to coat both sides.

Transfer the coated breasts to a baking sheet and bake for 30 minutes until the chicken is golden and cooked through. Remove the cocktail sticks before serving.

Chicken Kiev

Chicken Kiev has been a favorite for hundreds of years, thanks to its crispy coating and oozing buttery garlic center. Invented by a Russian chef, it was once fancily named Côtelettes de Volaille, and even formed part of Queen Victoria's Christmas Day menu in 1899.

2 tablespoons olive oil

4 chicken thighs, skin on

1 garlic clove, finely chopped

1 tablespoon sweet paprika

pinch of saffron threads

4oz string beans, trimmed and sliced into 1½ inch lengths

2 tomatoes, finely chopped

1 (13oz) can cannellini beans, rinsed and drained

6 canned artichoke hearts, finely chopped

2 rosemary sprigs, finely chopped, plus extra sprigs to garnish

1 teaspoon salt

2½ cups water

scant 1¼ cups Bomba or Calasparra rice

Heat the oil in a 12 inch paella pan or skillet over medium-high heat. Add the chicken thighs and cook for 2 minutes on each side until browned.

Add the garlic, sweet paprika, saffron, string beans, and tomatoes, reduce the heat to medium, and cook gently for 2 minutes. Stir in the cannellini beans, artichokes, rosemary, and salt, then gradually pour in the measurement water. Add the rice and stir, increasing the heat a little until the liquid starts to bubble.

Simmer without stirring for about 10 minutes, then flip the chicken pieces over and cook for another 10 minutes, or until the chicken is cooked through and the rice has absorbed most of the liquid—the rice will gradually form a crust at the bottom (the socarrat, considered a particular delicacy).

Remove the pan from the heat and let stand for 5 minutes. Garnish the chicken with extra sprigs of rosemary, then carry the pan to the table to serve.

Chicken Paella

Tradition dictates that paella should be made in an enormously wide pan on an open fire, by a man. I've obviously broken all the rules by making mine in a 12 inch skillet in my kitchen, but feel free to stick to the traditions as you see fit. The rice is important: paella rices like Bomba and Calasparra swell while keeping their grains distinct; risotto rices become creamy. If you can't find paella rice, use a generic short-grain rice instead.

3½oz gluten-free white bread

2 teaspoons paprika

1 tablespoon gluten-free vegetable stock powder

1 egg

4 boneless, skinless chicken breasts, about 5oz each, cut into ¾ inch cubes

2 teaspoons sunflower oil

VARIATION

You can make these nuggets dairy-free, too: use stock powder and bread that are dairy-free as well as gluten-free, and use soy milk if you want to presoak the chicken breasts.

Preheat the oven to 325°F.

Place the bread in a food processor and pulse to form bread crumbs. Spread out the crumbs in a roasting pan and bake for about 30 minutes, stirring occasionally, until dried out and browned.

Transfer the dried bread crumbs to a food processor, add the paprika and vegetable stock powder and pulse a few times until the mixture resembles sand. Pour it into a large plastic bag and set aside.

Beat the egg in a medium-size bowl. Add the chicken to the bowl in batches, stirring to ensure each piece is evenly coated. Lift the pieces out with a slotted spoon and drop them into the bag with the crumb mixture. Hold the bag firmly shut and then shake it to coat the chicken. Lift out each piece using tongs. Repeat until all the chicken has been coated. (The nuggets can either be frozen or cooked at this stage.)

Increase the oven temperature to 350°F. Drizzle the oil onto a baking sheet. Place the nuggets on the sheet, then stir them around slightly until lightly coated in the oil. Bake for about 15 minutes (or 20–25 minutes from frozen) until the coating is golden and the chicken is cooked through.

Chicken Nuggets

These chicken nuggets are surprisingly quick and easy to make and require no deep-frying. The uncooked nuggets freeze well, too. You can serve them with French fries or potato wedges, but they also make a great meal served with gluten-free spaghetti and Simple Tomato Sauce (see page 170). If you want extra-juicy nuggets, soak the chicken breasts in milk overnight before you chop them up.

1½ tablespoons olive oil

1 onion, finely chopped

4 garlic cloves, finely chopped

1 red chile, seeded and cut into very thin strips

1 teaspoon gluten-free ground cinnamon

1 (14oz) can coconut milk

1 tablespoon tomato paste

juice of 1 lime

1lb boneless, skinless chicken breasts, cut into thin strips

1 teaspoon soft dark brown sugar

6 cherry tomatoes, halved

3½oz fine green beans, trimmed

1½ cups chopped cilantro

salt

Heat the oil in a large pan over medium heat, add the onion, garlic, chile, and cinnamon, and fry gently for about 5 minutes until the onion has softened.

Stir in half the coconut milk, the tomato paste, and lime juice, then add the chicken, sugar, and cherry tomatoes. Bring to a boil, then reduce the heat and simmer gently, uncovered, for about 15 minutes, or until the chicken is cooked through. Season to taste with salt.

Add the green beans to the pan, then gradually stir in the remaining coconut milk until the sauce is the consistency of cream. Cook for another 5 minutes, then remove the pan from the heat and stir in the chopped cilantro.

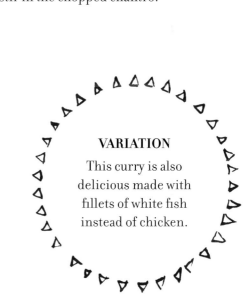

VARIATION
This curry is also delicious made with fillets of white fish instead of chicken.

Coconut & Lime Chicken Curry

This chicken curry is inspired by flavors commonly used in dishes from Thailand and the west coast of India: garlic, tomato, lime, and coconut, all mixed up with plenty of fresh cilantro. Serve it with boiled white rice or jasmine rice.

SERVES 4–6

1 quantity gluten-free Plain Short Pastry Crust dough (see page 166)

cornstarch, for dusting

4 teaspoons tomato paste

2 teaspoons olive oil

6 smoked lean bacon slices, cut into small pieces

4oz broccoli, roughly chopped

3 eggs

¾ cup light cream

6 tablespoons milk

salt and pepper

Preheat the oven to 350°F.

Roll out the dough to about ¼ inch thick on a counter well dusted with cornstarch. Line an 8 inch tart pan with the dough and trim any excess using a sharp knife. Spread the tomato paste over the base of the pastry shell, then sprinkle with a little salt.

Heat the oil in a nonstick skillet, add the bacon, and fry for about 5 minutes until any water has evaporated and it is golden brown and slightly crunchy.

Meanwhile, boil or steam the broccoli until very tender. Drain, if necessary, and let cool slightly, then finely chop.

Scatter the cooked bacon and broccoli over the pastry shell.

Beat the eggs in a pitcher, then whisk in the cream, milk, and a little salt and pepper. Pour into the pastry shell and bake for 30 minutes until browned and the filling is completely set.

Broccoli & Bacon Quiche

This quiche can be eaten hot or cold—personally, I think it goes really well with arugula leaves and some potato salad on the side.

SERVES 4

5oz gluten-free white bread

2 teaspoons paprika

1 tablespoon gluten-free
vegetable stock powder

1 egg

1¼lb pork loin chops, trimmed

2 tablespoons sunflower oil

Preheat the oven to 325°F.

Place the bread in a food processor and pulse to form bread crumbs. Spread out the crumbs in a roasting pan and bake for about 20 minutes, stirring occasionally, until dried out.

Place the crisp crumbs in the food processor with the paprika and vegetable stock powder. Pulse a few times to form a sandlike mixture. Tip onto a large plate. Beat the egg on another large plate.

One at a time, place each pork chop between 2 sheets of plastic wrap or baking paper, then bang vigorously with a rolling pin until no more than ½ inch thick.

Using a fork, dip the pork pieces in the egg, then in the bread crumbs, turning until well coated on both sides.

Heat the sunflower oil in a nonstick skillet over medium heat and fry the scallops for 3–4 minutes on each side or until cooked through, crispy, and golden brown. Drain on paper towels and serve hot or cold.

VARIATION

To make a dairy-free version of this recipe, choose bread and stock powder that are dairy-free as well as gluten-free.

Breaded Pork Scallops

Whether you call them scallops or schnitzel, these thin pieces of breaded pork make excellent sandwich fillings, or can simply be served with a wedge of lemon and a sprinkling of parsley.

3lb boned ham joint

1 pineapple

3 tablespoons soft dark brown sugar

2 teaspoons gluten-free mustard

1 teaspoon cornstarch

2 tablespoons orange juice

Place the ham in a large stockpot or saucepan and cover with cold water. Let soak overnight, then discard the water.

Cover the ham with fresh water and bring to a boil, then reduce the heat and simmer for 45 minutes until the ham is cooked through, skimming the surface with a metal spoon. Drain the ham and let cool slightly.

Meanwhile, cut away the pineapple skin and leaves and remove the core—if you want classic pineapple rings, use a pineapple corer or small serrated knife. Finely dice 2oz of the pineapple and set aside. Slice the remainder into pieces about $\frac{1}{2}$ inch thick, then arrange in a roasting pan.

Place the diced pineapple in a small saucepan, add the brown sugar, mustard, and cornstarch and heat gently until the mixture thickens. Set aside.

Preheat the oven to 350°F. Place the cooled ham on a cutting board and remove any string. Using a very sharp knife, remove the skin and most of the fat until a $\frac{1}{8}$ inch layer of fat remains. Score this into a diamond pattern with the tip of the knife. You may want to retie some cook's string around the ham. Place the ham on the sliced pineapple in the roasting pan.

Spread a thick layer of the diced pineapple mixture over the top of the ham, then roast for 45–60 minutes until the top is darkened and sticky. Remove from the oven and place on a carving board.

Add the orange juice to the juices in the roasting pan and stir well. Slice the ham and serve with the roast pineapple and a drizzle of orange sauce.

Roast Pineapple & Mustard Ham

Pineapple, brown sugar, and mustard create a spicy, chewy topping for a roast joint of ham and also form the basis of a tangy orange sauce to serve alongside. It's wonderful for a special occasion, but also easy enough to make for a regular weekend.

SERVES 4–6

2 carrots, peeled and roughly chopped

2 celery sticks, roughly chopped

1 onion, quartered

2 tablespoons olive oil

1¾lb lean ground beef

2 (13oz) cans chopped tomatoes

¼ cup gluten-free ketchup

¼ cup red wine

¼ teaspoon salt

3 zucchini, about 13oz total weight

2 tablespoons unsalted butter

2½ tablespoons cornstarch

1½ cups milk

½ cup grated cheddar cheese

Place the carrots, celery, and onion in a food processor and blitz until finely ground. Alternatively, chop the vegetables very finely.

Heat half the oil in a saucepan, add the beef, and fry for about 10 minutes, breaking it up with a wooden spoon, until browned and cooked through. Drain off any liquid and transfer the beef to a bowl. Set aside.

Heat the remaining oil in the pan, add the ground vegetables, and fry gently for about 5 minutes until softened. Add the cooked beef, tomatoes, ketchup, wine, and salt and simmer for 1 hour.

Meanwhile, slice the zucchini lengthwise into very thin ribbons (use a mandolin, if you have one), then steam until just tender and drain.

When you are ready to assemble the lasagna, preheat the oven to 325°F. Melt the butter in a saucepan, then stir in the cornstarch and whisk until lump-free. Gradually add the milk, stirring until smooth. Bring to a boil, whisking continuously until the sauce is thickened.

Spread half the meat mixture in a 12 x 9 inch lasagna dish and cover with half the zucchini strips. Repeat with the remaining meat and zucchini. Pour over the white sauce and sprinkle the cheese on top. Bake for 50 minutes until the cheese is browned.

Low-carb Lasagna

Few dishes are as appealing as homecooked lasagna, straight from the oven. Even better, thinly sliced zucchini takes the place of pasta for this version, making it very low in carbohydrates.

2 teaspoons cornstarch

1 (15oz) can pineapple chunks in juice

¼ cup gluten-free ketchup

1 tablespoon cider vinegar

1 teaspoon salt

2 balls preserved ginger from a jar of preserved ginger in syrup, finely diced

2 tablespoons olive oil

13oz pork, trimmed and cut into pencil-thick strips

1 onion, sliced

8 scallions, cut diagonally into ¾ inch lengths

1 yellow bell pepper, cored, seeded, and cut into thin sticks

1 carrot, peeled and cut into thin sticks

4 garlic cloves, finely chopped

3½oz snow peas, trimmed

Place the cornstarch in a pitcher and gradually stir in all the juice from the can of pineapple. Add the ketchup, vinegar, salt, and 1 tablespoon syrup from the preserved ginger jar and mix well.

Heat the oil in a wok or large skillet until it is hot. Add the pork, onion, scallions, yellow bell pepper, carrot, garlic, and preserved ginger and stir-fry for 2 minutes, or until the pork is just cooked through. Stir in the cornstarch mixture and cook for another few minutes.

Stir in the pineapple chunks and snow peas and continue to stir-fry for 2 minutes ,or until heated through, then serve immediately.

Sweet & Sour Pork

Prepared Chinese sauces almost always contain soy sauce, which also contains wheat flour. This quick and easy sweet and sour pork is full of colorful, crunchy vegetables and is made without soy sauce, but you'd never notice the difference. Serve with rice.

8 fat leeks

2 teaspoons olive oil

13oz pancetta or
chopped bacon

1 cup ricotta cheese

2 (13oz) cans chopped tomatoes

2 (8oz) balls buffalo mozzarella
cheese, torn into chunks

2 teaspoons dried oregano

sea salt

Preheat the oven to 350°F.

Trim the leeks and remove the outer layer. Rinse out as
much grit as you can without cutting into the leeks. Fit the
leeks into a stockpot or large pan, cover with boiling water,
and cook for about 10 minutes until soft. Drain and rinse
under cold running water until cool enough to handle, then
push out the centers to form 8 leek tubes. Take the 4 fattest
removed centers and push out the centers again to form
another 4 leek tubes. Set the 12 tubes to one side and put
the cooked leek centers in a food processor.

Heat the oil in a skillet, add the pancetta or bacon, and cook
for 4–5 minutes until well cooked, but not crispy. Add to the
food processor with the ricotta. Pulse a few times until fully
chopped but retaining some texture—you don't want a puree.

Scoop the mixture into a plastic food bag and cut off one of
the corners, then pipe into the leek tubes.

Place the filled leeks in a large ovenproof dish and top with
the tomatoes. Half-fill 1 empty tomato can with water and
add to the dish. Scatter over the mozzarella, followed by
the dried oregano and a sprinkling of salt.

Bake for 35–40 minutes until heated through and the
mozzarella is golden brown. Serve.

Leek & Pancetta Cannelloni

If you push the centers out of large leeks you end up with thin
tubes that are a nutritious substitute for cannelloni pasta. They
have the bonus of being very low in carbohydrates. The leek
tubes can be used for a variety of fillings, but for this recipe
I've mixed the remainder of the leek with pancetta and ricotta
to make an Italian-inspired bake.

sunflower oil, for greasing

3½oz gluten-free bread, crusts removed

¼ cup milk

13oz lean ground beef

1 teaspoon salt

½ teaspoon gluten-free ground allspice

½ teaspoon ground black pepper

Preheat the oven to 350°F. Generously grease a baking sheet with sunflower oil.

Roughly crumble the bread into a large bowl and add the milk. Stir together until smooth and well mixed. Add the beef, salt, allspice, and pepper and, using your hands, mix together well.

Roll about 1 tablespoon of the meat mixture into a ball and place on the prepared baking sheet. Repeat with the remaining mixture to make about 35 meatballs. Roll the meatballs around on the sheet to coat lightly in the oil.

Bake for 25–30 minutes until crisp on the outside and soft but cooked through inside. Serve hot.

Swedish Meatballs

Swedish meatballs are characterized by their softness, the secret of which is bread crumbs soaked in milk. Serve Swedish-style, with gravy made by stirring ¼ cup light cream into 1 cup thickened beef gravy (add salt to taste), boiled new potatoes, and a dollop of lingonberry or cranberry sauce alongside. Alternatively, try them on gluten-free spaghetti with Simple Tomato Sauce (see page 170).

SERVES 6

1 tablespoon olive oil

1 small onion, finely chopped

1lb ground beef

3½oz mushrooms, diced

1 red bell pepper, cored, seeded, and diced

1 tablespoon smoked paprika

2 teaspoons chopped oregano

1 teaspoon gluten-free instant coffee

1 small green chile, seeded and finely chopped (optional)

1 (13oz) can kidney beans, rinsed and drained

2 (13oz) cans chopped tomatoes

¼ cup water

Heat the oil in a large saucepan, add the onion, and fry gently for 5 minutes until softened. Add the beef and cook for about 10 minutes, breaking it up with a spoon, until browned and almost cooked through.

Add the mushrooms and red bell pepper, then stir in the smoked paprika, oregano, coffee, and green chile, if using. Add the kidney beans, tomatoes, and measurement water (rinse out the empty tomato cans with the water before adding), then stir well and bring to a boil.

Reduce the heat to medium-low, cover with a lid, and simmer for 2 hours, stirring occasionally, to let the flavors develop.

Chili

Chili is real one-pot food, great for those times when you want to keep preparation to a minimum. This version uses smoked paprika, oregano, and coffee to make a rich sauce that isn't too hot, but if you're not fond of spicy food, just omit the chile. Serve with corn tacos or homemade Corn Tortillas (see page 179).

MAKES 6

1 onion, quartered

13oz lean ground beef

¼ teaspoon salt

¼ teaspoon ground black pepper

olive oil, for frying (optional)

Place the onion in a food processor and blitz until ground, then tip into a bowl with the beef and mix together. Add the salt and pepper, then mix together using your hands.

Divide the mixture into 6 equal-size portions and shape into patties about ½ inch thick.

You can now either shallow-fry the burgers in a little olive oil or barbecue them until cooked through. About 2–3 minutes on each side is usually sufficient. To check if the burgers are cooked through, cut one open—no pink should remain.

Beefburgers

Store-bought beefburgers often have wheat flour as an added ingredient, making them unsuitable for people avoiding gluten. Luckily, burgers are surprisingly quick and easy to make at home. Use good-quality beef and there's no need for fillers.

SWEET

SERVES 4–6

7 tablespoons unsalted butter, melted, plus extra for greasing

¾ cup plus 1 teaspoon Gluten-Free Plain White Flour Blend (see page 164)

½ cup granulated sugar

½ cup dry unsweetened coconut

1 teaspoon gluten-free baking powder

pinch of salt

1 egg, lightly beaten

2 cooking apples, about 13oz total weight, peeled, cored, and sliced

2 teaspoons raw brown sugar

1 teaspoon gluten-free ground cinnamon

Preheat the oven to 325°F. Grease a 9 inch springform cake pan with butter.

Place the flour blend, sugar, coconut, baking powder, and salt in a bowl. Pour the melted butter into the dry ingredients and stir well. Add the egg and mix until well combined.

Spread the batter evenly in the prepared cake pan. Arrange the apples on top and sprinkle with the raw brown sugar and cinnamon. Bake for 50 minutes until the apples are golden and the base is shrinking from the sides of the pan. (The tart will be quite delicate when hot, but becomes more robust as it cools.) Serve warm or cold.

VARIATION

Use 7 tablespoons dairy-free margarine instead of butter for a dairy-free version of this recipe.

Apple & Coconut Tart

My mother's friend Rie introduced me to this quick and easy tart. I immediately fell in love with its sharp apple topping and the subtly coconut-flavored base that is crunchy on the outside and chewy within. Serve warm or cold with crème fraîche.

4oz gluten-free sweet
plain hard cookies

5 tablespoons unsalted butter

½ teaspoon gluten-free
ground ginger

¾ cup cream cheese

½ cup light cream

¾ cup confectioners' sugar, sifted

pinch of salt

2 eggs, separated

Rhubarb sauce

11½oz rhubarb, trimmed and cut
into ½ inch pieces

¼ cup granulated sugar, plus extra
if needed

¼ cup water

2 balls from a jar of preserved
ginger in syrup, about 1oz,
finely diced

Place the cookies in a sealed plastic food bag and bash with
a rolling pin to form crumbs. Alternatively, blitz them in a
food processor. Melt 3½ tablespoons of the butter in a small
saucepan, then stir in the cookie crumbs and ground ginger
until well combined. Tip the crumbs into a deep 8 inch loose-
bottomed tart pan or springform pan and smooth the mixture
level using the back of a metal tablespoon.

Preheat the oven to 400°F. To make the filling, melt the
remaining butter and pour into a large bowl. Add the cream
cheese and stir until smooth. Gradually add the cream, followed
by the confectioners' sugar and salt.

Stir the egg yolks into the cream cheese mixture. Whisk the
egg whites in a thoroughly clean bowl until they form firm
peaks, then fold into the cheese mixture.

Pour the mixture onto the cookie base and bake for 10 minutes,
then reduce the oven temperature to 325°F and cook for another
35 minutes until a skewer inserted into the center comes out
clean and the cheesecake is risen and browned. (The filling will
sink as it cools, but this is normal.)

To make the sauce, place all the ingredients in a saucepan and
simmer gently for about 15 minutes until the rhubarb is tender
and starting to disintegrate, but retains some texture. Add a
little more sugar to the sauce, if liked. Serve the sauce hot or
cold with the warm or chilled cheesecake. To serve the cake
chilled, transfer it to a large plate. If serving the cake warm,
leave it in the tart pan, as it's tricky to transfer.

Baked Cheesecake
with Rhubarb & Ginger

Based on a traditional American recipe, this cheesecake has
a dark, undulating crust and a slightly wobbly center. Its creamy
flavor and soufflé-like texture marry well with the spiced rhubarb
sauce—I love the bright pink of new-season rhubarb, in particular.

1¼ sticks plus 1 tablespoon
unsalted butter,
plus extra for greasing

¾ cup granulated sugar

½ cup water

1 teaspoon vanilla extract

1⅔ cups Gluten-Free Plain White
Flour Blend (see page 164)

¾ cup ground almonds

2 teaspoons gluten-free
baking powder

pinch of salt

4 eggs, lightly beaten

confectioners' sugar, for dusting

Filling

½ cup whipping cream

1 cup strawberries, hulled

2 tablespoons strawberry jam

Preheat the oven to 300°F. Lightly grease 2 x 8 inch sandwich pans with butter.

Place the butter, sugar, measurement water, and vanilla extract in a saucepan and cook over medium-high heat until the butter melts. Add the flour blend and then whisk continuously—the mixture will thicken and may stick to the bottom of the pan, so keep whisking to prevent it burning (don't worry about small lumps at this stage). When a thick paste forms, remove the pan from the heat, and keep whisking for another 20 seconds, then set aside.

In a large bowl, stir together the ground almonds, baking powder, and salt. Pour in the paste and add the eggs. Whisk together for 1 minute (use a handheld electric whisk if you have one), then divide the batter evenly between the cake pans. Bake for 25 minutes until risen, golden, and a skewer inserted into the center comes out clean. Let cool in the pans.

Whip the cream until soft peaks form. Set aside 2 tablespoons of the cream and 8 strawberries for decoration. Slice the remaining strawberries and stir into the jam.

Spread the cream across the top of one cake, followed by the strawberry mixture. Sandwich together with the remaining cake and dust with confectioners' sugar. Decorate with the reserved cream and strawberries.

Strawberry Sponge Cake

This cake uses a slightly unusual method, but the result is a light and extremely soft vanilla sponge that is perfectly matched by the filling of cream, jam, and fresh strawberries.

MAKES ABOUT 12 SLICES

5 tablespoons unsalted butter, softened, plus extra for greasing

½ cup granulated sugar

2 eggs, lightly beaten

½ cup brown rice flour

¾ cup ground almonds

2 teaspoons gluten-free baking powder

grated zest of 2 unwaxed lemons

1 tablespoon milk

Topping

juice of 1 lemon

¼ cup granulated sugar

Preheat the oven to 340°F. Lightly grease a 9 inch loaf pan with butter.

Place the butter and sugar in a bowl and beat together for about 1 minute with a handheld electric whisk until light and fluffy. Add the eggs, rice flour, ground almonds, and baking powder and beat together for a few seconds until combined. Add the lemon zest and milk, then beat again.

Spoon the batter into the prepared pan and shake slightly to make sure the batter is evenly distributed. Bake for 40 minutes until a skewer inserted into the center comes out clean.

Meanwhile, mix together the lemon juice and sugar in a cup (the sugar won't dissolve, but that is normal).

Leaving the cake in the pan, lightly prick the top all over with a fork, then evenly pour over the lemon juice mixture while the cake is still hot. Let cool in the pan before serving.

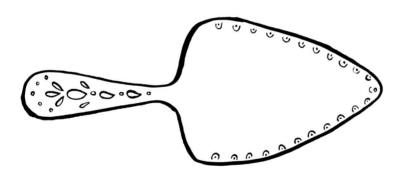

Lemon Drizzle Cake

The combination of crunchy sugar topping and lemon-soaked sponge makes this loaf cake a perennial teatime favorite; it is also a fine dessert if you serve each slice with a scoop of raspberry sorbet. It'll keep for a couple of days in an airtight container.

5 tablespoons unsalted butter, diced, plus extra for greasing

12oz gooseberries, trimmed

⅓ cup granulated sugar

¼ cup elderflower cordial

½ cup plain yogurt

1⅔ cups ground almonds

⅔ cup cornmeal

2 eggs, lightly beaten

1 teaspoon baking soda

1 teaspoon gluten-free baking powder

pinch of salt

Icing

½ cup confectioners' sugar, sifted

2 teaspoons elderflower cordial

1 teaspoon lemon juice

Preheat the oven to 350°F. Lightly grease a 9 inch springform cake pan with butter.

Place the gooseberries, sugar, and cordial in a saucepan over medium heat and gently cook until the sugar has dissolved and the fruit is tender. Let cool for about 10 minutes, then puree with a handheld blender or in a food processor or blender. Stir in the butter and let melt.

Pour the mixture into a large bowl, add the yogurt, ground almonds, cornmeal, eggs, baking soda, baking powder, and salt and stir until combined. Quickly spoon the batter into the prepared pan and bake for 40 minutes until well browned and firm to the touch. Let cool completely in the pan.

To make the icing, mix together the confectioners' sugar, cordial, and lemon juice in a bowl. Run a knife around the edges of the pan and transfer the cake to a serving plate. Drizzle over the icing and let set for at least 1 hour before serving.

Gooseberry & Elderflower Cake

With its combination of juicy gooseberries and fragrant elderflower, this moist and simple cake captures the essence of a warm day. But it need not be summer when you make it because it works just as well with frozen berries and cordial from the pantry. It'll keep for a couple of days in an airtight container.

2 tablespoons sunflower oil, plus extra for greasing

1½ cups walnut pieces, plus 3 walnut halves to decorate

½ cup brown rice flour

¼ cup packed dark brown sugar

½ cup milk

2 eggs, lightly beaten

1 teaspoon vanilla extract

2 teaspoons instant coffee

3 teaspoons boiling water

2 teaspoons gluten-free baking powder

Buttercream

1 teaspoon instant coffee

2 teaspoons boiling water

¾ cup confectioners' sugar, sifted

3½ tablespoons unsalted butter, softened

Icing

½ teaspoon instant coffee

2 teaspoons boiling water

½ cup confectioners' sugar, sifted

Preheat the oven to 340°F. Lightly oil a 9 inch loaf pan with sunflower oil.

Place 100g (3½oz) of the walnut pieces and the rice flour in a food processor and process until the mixture is the texture of coffee grinds. Add the brown sugar, milk, oil, eggs, and vanilla extract. Stir together the instant coffee and measurement boiling water in a small cup until the coffee dissolves. Pour into the food processor and blend for 1 minute until the mixture is thick and creamy. Let stand for 15 minutes.

Add the baking powder to the cake batter and blend for a couple of seconds. Fold in the remaining walnut pieces, then pour into the prepared loaf pan, smoothing the top with a spatula. Bake for 30 minutes until an inserted skewer comes out clean. Let cool in the pan.

To make the buttercream filling, mix together the coffee and measurement boiling water in a large bowl, then stir in the confectioners' sugar. Add the butter and beat until well combined.

Cut the cooled cake in half horizontally using a sharp knife (I find a bread knife works best). Evenly spread the base with the buttercream, then sandwich together with the top.

To make the icing, mix together the coffee and measurement boiling water in a bowl until completely dissolved (or you'll get dark flecks in your icing). Stir in the confectioners' sugar to form a thick mixture. Spread across the top of the cake using a palette knife, then decorate with the walnut halves. Chill for 1 hour before serving.

Coffee & Walnut Cake

Coffee and walnut is a wonderful flavor combination. I've used ground walnuts in place of much of the flour, which makes this cake a more nutritious treat. The natural oiliness of the walnuts reduces the need for added fats.

4 cooking apples, about 1¾lb total weight, peeled, cored, and cut into small chunks

2 teaspoons water

4 teaspoons granulated sugar, plus extra if needed

7 tablespoons unsalted butter

½ cup packed light brown sugar

8 cups gluten-free cornflakes

Place the apples, measurement water, and granulated sugar in a saucepan and cook over low heat for about 15–20 minutes until the apples have softened and are still a little sour but not eye-wateringly so—add more sugar to taste if necessary. Let cool.

Meanwhile, melt the butter in a large skillet over low heat, add the brown sugar, and stir until the sugar dissolves. Increase the heat slightly and add the cornflakes. Using a spoon, crush them gently and stir for a few minutes until well coated in the butter mixture. Let cool, stirring occasionally to prevent the flakes clumping together.

To serve, alternate layers of apple and cornflakes evenly among 4 dessert glasses. Serve immediately.

Crunchy Cornflake Apple Pudding

Buttery, toffee-flavored crunchy cornflakes are layered sundae-style with soft and slightly tart stewed apple in this tasty dessert. It's one of my mother's inventions and is a regular feature of fall at home, thanks to the tree in the garden. While the apple and buttered cornflakes can be made in advance, the dessert needs to be assembled just before it is served or you'll end up with a soggy mess. Delicious with crème fraîche or whipped cream.

MAKES 6

½ cup tapioca flour

½ cup milk

¼ cup lukewarm water

1 teaspoon active dry yeast

2 teaspoons granulated sugar

⅔ cup Gluten-Free Plain
White Flour Blend (see page 164),
plus extra for dusting

½ cup ground almonds

2 teaspoons sunflower oil

pinch of salt

2 tablespoons unsalted butter,
softened

3 tablespoons light brown sugar

1 teaspoon gluten-free ground
cinnamon

Place the tapioca flour and milk in a saucepan and heat
gently, stirring, until it comes together as a very sticky
white lump. Remove the pan from the heat.

Stir together the warm measurement water, yeast, and
granulated sugar in a cup and let stand for a few minutes
until the mixture starts to froth.

Place the flour blend, ground almonds, oil, and salt in
a large bowl. Pour in the yeasty liquid, then add the tapioca
mixture to the bowl and, using a spoon, turn the lump over
until it is well coated in flour. Knead together for at least
1 minute until well combined and the dough is slightly oily.
Turn the dough out onto a counter lightly dusted with
flour blend and spread out to a rough rectangle, about
9½ x 7 inches.

Mix together the butter, brown sugar, and cinnamon in
a small bowl, then spread the mixture evenly across the
dough. Starting at one of the narrow ends, roll up the
dough and cut into 6 slices.

Place the circles, spiral side up, in a small roasting pan,
about 7 x 5 inches. Loosely cover the dish with plastic wrap
and let rise in a warm place for at least 1½ hours until the
slices have puffed up and filled the pan.

Preheat the oven to 325°F. Bake the buns for 40 minutes
until golden brown. Serve warm.

Cinnamon Spiral Buns

The smell of sweet cinnamon buns baking is the epitome
of coziness—and probably why they are so popular across
Scandinavia. If you want to eat these for breakfast, I recommend
making them the night before and baking them for 30 minutes;
the final 10 minutes of baking can then be carried out in the
morning in order to enjoy them fresh from the oven.

SERVES 6

butter, for greasing

2 teaspoons granulated sugar

13oz fresh cherries,
rinsed and pitted

⅓ cup cornstarch

1 cup light cream,
plus extra to serve

½ cup ground almonds

⅓ cup packed light brown sugar

4 eggs

¼ teaspoon almond extract

pinch of salt

Preheat the oven to 340°F. Grease a pie dish with butter, then sprinkle with the granulated sugar.

Pat the cherries dry using paper towels, then scatter across the pie dish.

Place the cornstarch and cream in a bowl and whisk together until smooth. Add the ground almonds, brown sugar, eggs, almond extract, and salt. Whisk to combine, then pour into the dish.

Bake for 50–60 minutes until risen, puffy, and well browned.

Cherry Clafoutis

Clafoutis is a French dessert featuring fresh cherries baked in a delicious sweet batter—so delicious, in fact, that I am always torn between the joy of eating the cherries raw or cooking them like this. It is definitely one of my top 10 desserts. Serve warm with cream.

SERVES 2

1 English Breakfast tea bag

1½ cups boiling water

1 cup gluten-free rolled oats, quinoa flakes, or millet flakes

½ cup apple juice

1 (13oz) can prunes in juice

5 teaspoons sunflower seeds

Steep the tea bag in the measurement boiling water for 2 minutes, then pour into a saucepan. Discard the tea bag.

Add the oats, quinoa, or millet, the apple juice, and the juice from the can of prunes and simmer over medium heat for about 10 minutes, stirring occasionally, until the mixture thickens.

Stir in the prunes and cook for another 1 minute, then pour into 2 serving bowls and sprinkle over the sunflower seeds.

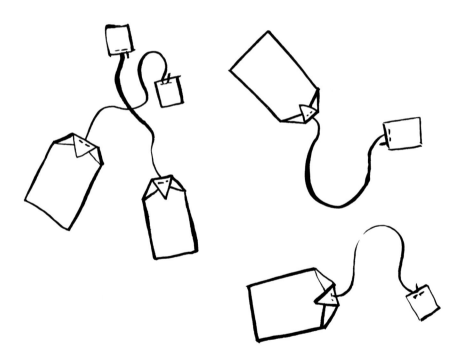

Prune Oatmeal

Prunes combine with English Breakfast tea to flavor a nutritious oatmeal of oats, millet, or quinoa (my favorite), as you prefer. Just remember to watch out for prune pits!

1 cup gluten-free
rolled oats

½ cup good-quality
apple juice

½ cup water

½ cup plain yogurt

1 dessert apple, cored and
coarsely grated

5 teaspoons sunflower seeds

⅛ cup walnut pieces

1 teaspoon flaxseeds

Place the oats in a large bowl, add the apple juice and measurement water, and let soak overnight.

The next morning, stir in the yogurt. Add the apple and sprinkle over the sunflower seeds, then stir together.

Spoon the muesli into 2 bowls and sprinkle over the walnut pieces and flaxseeds.

VARIATION

Red currants, raspberries, blueberries, or pomegranate seeds all taste great sprinkled on top if you want a bit of variation. For a dairy-free breakfast, use soy yogurt instead of the plain yogurt.

Bircher Muesli

Bircher muesli makes a nutritious start to the day and, apart from a little forethought (the oats need to soak overnight), is dead easy to make, and you can dress it up or down as you wish.

¼ cup clear honey

2 tablespoons sunflower oil

1 teaspoon gluten-free baking
powder

2¾ cups gluten-free plain
puffed rice

½ cup quinoa flakes

½ cup sunflower seeds

½ cup pumpkin seeds

⅓ cup chopped walnuts

⅓ cup chopped hazelnuts

Preheat the oven to 325°F.

Mix together the honey, oil, and baking powder in a small bowl.
Place the puffed rice, quinoa flakes, sunflower seeds, and
pumpkin seeds in a large roasting pan. Pour over the honey
mixture and stir until all the dry ingredients are well coated.

Roast for 15 minutes, then stir again. Return the pan to the oven
and cook for another 10 minutes.

Add the nuts to the granola while it is still warm. Give it another
good stir and let cool. It will keep for 2 weeks stored in an
airtight container.

Honey-Roast Granola

A touch of honey makes this nutritious granola especially tasty.
I love it because it's not only simple to make but also versatile.
I've used walnuts and hazelnuts here, but don't feel limited by this:
they can easily be substituted with the same weight of other
nuts or dried fruit, depending on your preferences and pantry
contents (Brazil nuts and chopped dried apricots are another
great pairing). Try the granola drenched with apple or orange
juice for a dairy-free breakfast.

**MAKES ABOUT 8
SERVINGS**

½ cup quinoa flakes

¼ cup sunflower seeds

¼ cup clear honey

1 tablespoon cider vinegar

2 tablespoons sunflower oil

4 teaspoons unsweetened cocoa

pinch of salt

3¼ cups gluten-free cornflakes

2 cups gluten-free plain
puffed rice

⅔ cup raisins

Preheat the oven to 325°F.

Spread the quinoa flakes and sunflower seeds over a baking
sheet and bake for 30 minutes.

Meanwhile, place the honey and vinegar in a large saucepan,
stir together, and bubble over medium heat for about
5 minutes until the mixture turns a rich brown—about the color
of a toffee apple. Remove the pan from the heat and quickly
stir in the oil, cocoa, and salt (the oil may not seem to mix in at
first, but everything should come together as you keep stirring).
The consistency should be similar to liquid chocolate—if the
mixture becomes too stiff, put the pan back over the heat for
a few seconds.

Tip in the toasted quinoa flakes and sunflower seeds, the
cornflakes, and puffed rice and stir until a mixture of flakes
and clumps is evenly coated.

Spread the granola onto a baking sheet and let cool completely,
then add the raisins.

VARIATION
To make this granola
extra special, coarsely
grate 1oz chocolate
(semisweet or milk as
you prefer) and add to
the cooled granola
with the raisins.

Choc Crunch Granola

This chocolate-flavored granola is perfect for those mornings
when you need a treat. It's fantastic with milk or as a topping
for yogurt, perhaps with some sliced banana as well. It will
keep for up to 2 weeks in an airtight container.

1 large banana, about 7½oz

1 dessert apple, about 3½oz, cored

½ cup rice flour

3½oz soft dried figs

1oz pitted prunes

2 tablespoons sunflower oil

1 teaspoon gluten-free baking powder

¼ cup dry unsweetened coconut

⅓ cup pumpkin seeds

Preheat the oven to 325°F.

Place the banana, apple, rice flour, figs, prunes, oil, and baking powder in a food processor or blender and blend until the apple is ground into small pieces and the mixture is thick but not too chunky.

Alternatively, grate the apple, mash the banana, and finely dice the figs and prunes, then mix together in a bowl. Stir in the rice flour, oil, and baking powder.

Add the coconut and pumpkin seeds and mix together well. Tip into a large loaf pan, smoothing the surface with the back of a spoon.

Bake for 30 minutes until cooked through and crispy on top. Let cool in the pan before cutting into slices.

Figgy Fruit Bars

These bars are packed with all manner of good things and have no added sugar, making them perfect for breakfast or as a snack when you're on the go. They'll keep for up to 3 days in an airtight container.

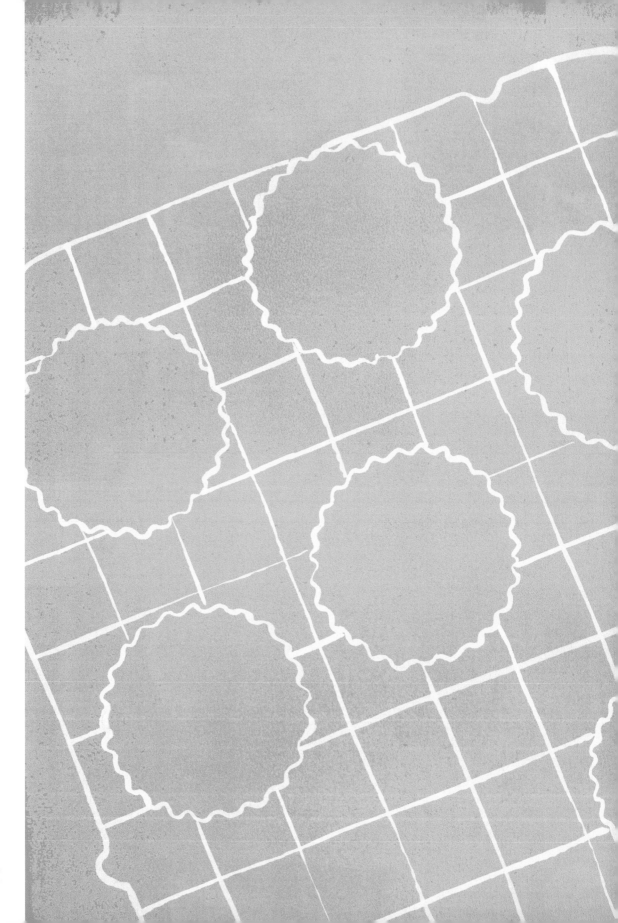

SMALL CAKES & COOKIES

1 quantity gluten-free Sweet Short Pastry Crust dough (see page 167)

cornstarch, for dusting

¼ cup sour cherry jam, such as Morello

2 tablespoons unsalted butter

3 tablespoons light brown sugar

¼ cup ground almonds

2½ tablespoons brown rice flour

1 egg, lightly beaten

¼ teaspoon almond extract

2 tablespoons slivered almonds

Preheat the oven to 350°F.

Roll out the dough to about ⅛ inch thick on a counter dusted with cornstarch. Stamp out 12 circles using a fluted pastry cutter a little larger than the sections of a 12-cup tart pan. Press the dough circles into the pan sections, then spoon ½ teaspoon of the jam into each pastry shell.

Melt the butter in a small saucepan, then stir in all the remaining ingredients except the slivered almonds. Spoon the mixture evenly over the tarts, taking care to ensure the jam is completely covered to prevent it oozing out during cooking.

Sprinkle ½ teaspoon of the slivered almonds over each tart. Bake for 20–25 minutes until golden brown and the pastry is cooked through. Let cool in the pan before serving.

VARIATION
Substitute the cherry jam with apricot or raspberry to give a different slant to this recipe.

Cherry Frangipane Tarts

These little tarts have soft domes of golden-brown almond frangipane that reveal a sour cherry jam center. Use a fluted pastry cutter for a professional look.

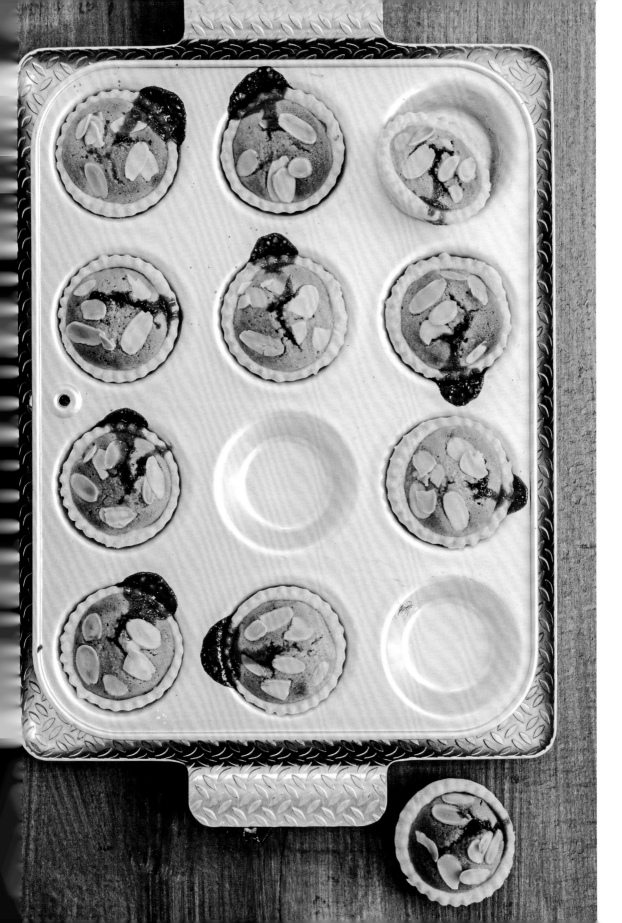

1 quantity gluten-free Sweet Short Pastry Crust dough (see page 167)

cornstarch, for dusting

¾ cup strawberry jam

VARIATION

I've specified strawberry jam, but other favorite jammy fillings are raspberry, black currant, blueberry, or apricot.

Preheat the oven to 350°F.

Roll out the dough to about ⅛ inch thick on a counter dusted with cornstarch. Stamp out 18 circles using a pastry cutter a little larger than the sections of a 12-cup tart pan. Press the dough circles into the sections of 2 x 12-cup tart pans, ensuring there are no holes or cracks in the dough for the jam to seep through.

Spoon 1 teaspoon of the jam into each pastry shell and bake for 30 minutes until the pastry is golden and cooked through. Transfer to a wire rack to cool—don't be tempted to eat these tarts straight from the oven because the jam will be very hot!

Jam Tarts

Jam tarts are great as a way of using up excess dough, as a fun project for the kids, or just because they taste fantastic! If you're making them with scraps of dough, the rule of thumb is 1 teaspoon of jam per tart—any more and the jam is likely to boil over and ooze all over the sheet, which is not only messy, but also makes it virtually impossible to extract the tarts whole.

150g (5oz) Gluten-Free Plain White Flour Blend (see page 164)

½ cup ground almonds

¾ cup granulated sugar

½ cup sunflower oil

3 eggs

2 teaspoons vanilla extract

pinch of salt

1½ cups fresh blueberries

1 teaspoon cornstarch

1 tablespoon gluten-free baking powder

Preheat the oven to 325°F. Line a 12-cup muffin pan with paper muffin liners.

Place the flour blend, ground almonds, sugar, oil, eggs, vanilla extract, and salt in a food processor and blend for 30 seconds to form a thick batter. Alternatively, whisk together in a bowl for 1 minute using a handheld electric whisk. Let the mixture stand for 15 minutes.

Meanwhile, toss the blueberries in the cornstarch until lightly covered (this helps to stop the blueberries sinking to the bottom of the muffins during cooking).

Add the baking powder to the muffin batter and blend briefly until combined. Add the blueberries and stir briefly (the blueberries don't need to be completely coated with batter).

Divide the batter evenly among the muffin liners and bake for 30 minutes until risen and golden. Let cool in the pan.

Blueberry Muffins

These moist and airy muffins are studded with gooey blueberries and are best eaten still slightly warm from the oven. They keep well for a couple of days, too (if there are any left!). Incidentally, my experiments have revealed that the movement of the blueberries during cooking is partly related to the size and shape of your muffin liners. If you find your blueberries are sinking to the bottom, just place the dusted blueberries on the top of the batter in the muffin liners before you bake, rather than folding them in. Bigger blueberries are also less likely to sink.

1¾ cups Gluten-Free Plain White Flour Blend (see page 164)

¾ cup granulated sugar

¾ cup milk

½ cup sunflower oil

3 eggs

grated zest of 2 large unwaxed oranges, plus extra to decorate

1 teaspoon vanilla extract

pinch of salt

2¼ tablespoons poppy seeds

1 tablespoon gluten-free baking powder

Icing

1 cup sifted confectioners' sugar

2½ teaspoons orange juice

Preheat the oven to 325°F. Line a 12-cup muffin pan with paper muffin liners.

Place the flour blend, sugar, milk, oil, eggs, orange zest, vanilla extract, and salt in a food processor and blend for 30 seconds to form a batter. Alternatively, whisk together in a bowl for 1 minute using a handheld electric whisk. Let the mixture stand for 20 minutes.

Add the poppy seeds and baking powder to the muffin batter and blend briefly until just combined. The batter will be runny, but this is fine.

Pour the batter evenly into the muffin liners and bake for 20 minutes until slightly golden. Let cool in the pan.

To make the icing, mix together the confectioners' sugar and orange juice in a bowl, then place a dollop on the top of each muffin. Grate a little orange zest over each muffin to decorate.

VARIATION

You can make a dairy-free version of this recipe by using soy milk in place of the milk.

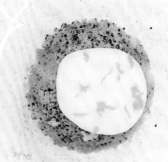

Orange Poppy Seed Muffins

These are the lightest, fluffiest muffins ever, with a lovely orange flavor and topped with a zingy citrus icing. The poppy seeds not only add an interesting texture to the muffins, they provide valuable fiber as well.

⅔ cup Gluten-Free Plain White Flour Blend (see page 164)

¼ cup plain yogurt

⅓ cup granulated sugar

2¼ tablespoons unsweetened cocoa

2 eggs

5 tablespoons unsalted butter, melted

1 teaspoon gluten-free baking powder

Chocolate icing

2¼ cups sifted confectioners' sugar

2 teaspoons unsweetened cocoa

2 tablespoons water

Creamy vanilla frosting

1⅛ sticks unsalted butter, softened

⅔ cup condensed milk

1½ cups sifted confectioners' sugar

1 teaspoon vanilla extract

Preheat the oven to 325°F. Line a 12-cup muffin pan with paper cake liners.

Place the flour blend, yogurt, sugar, cocoa, and eggs in a food processor. Add the melted butter and blend for 1 minute to form a batter. Alternatively, whisk together in a large bowl until well mixed. Let the batter stand for 20 minutes.

Whisk the baking powder into the cake batter, then divide evenly among the cake liners. Bake for 15 minutes until the cakes are just cooked through and a skewer inserted into the centers comes out clean. To keep the cakes moist, let cool in the pan under a clean dish towel.

To make the chocolate icing, mix together the ingredients in a bowl until smooth and thick, adding an extra ½ teaspoon water at a time if necessary—the icing should be thick enough that it can be spread onto the cakes without running down the sides.

To make the vanilla frosting, whisk together all the ingredients in a large bowl until well combined. Cover and chill for 30 minutes. Swirl or pipe the frosting onto your cakes as preferred, then chill the finished cakes until required.

Chocolate Cupcakes

This easy recipe gives light and delicious results every time.
Even better, these moist little cakes will keep for a couple of days,
so if necessary you can make them the day before you need them.
To quickly upgrade your cupcakes from ordinary to ooh-la-la, top them
with Chocolate Icing or Creamy Vanilla Frosting, and decorate with
candied cherries, chocolate chips, or gluten-free sugar sprinkles.

SMALL CAKES & COOKIES | 119

1½ sticks unsalted butter, melted, plus extra for greasing

2 cups brown rice flour

⅔ cup packed light brown sugar

½ cup granulated sugar

2 teaspoons vanilla extract

1 egg

½ cup chopped hazelnuts

¾ cup milk chocolate chips

Pour the melted butter into a food processor, add the rice flour, sugars, vanilla extract, and egg and blend for 1 minute to form a fairly stiff, pale brown dough. Let rest for 30 minutes to allow the rice flour to soften up and lose its grittiness.

Preheat the oven to 340°F. Lightly grease 2 baking sheets.

Scrape the cookie dough into a bowl and mix in the hazelnuts and chocolate chips. Place dessertspoonfuls of the dough onto the baking sheets, spaced well apart, and flatten slightly.

Bake for 13–15 minutes until golden brown and slightly spread out. Let cool on the sheets. Best eaten warm.

Chewy Chocolate Chip & Hazelnut Cookies

The science behind the perfect cookie is fascinating and I've discovered that not only is a high sugar content necessary to give a gooey middle, but even minor adjustments to egg, sugar, or flour quantities have a dramatic effect. It is all too easy to go from a chunky cookie with a chewy center to one with the look and texture of a very flat cake. This makes experimentation very difficult, but with this recipe a consistently good outcome can be achieved.

3½ tablespoons unsalted butter, softened, plus extra for greasing

⅔ cup granulated sugar

¾ cup Gluten-Free Plain White Flour Blend (see page 164)

1½ teaspoons gluten-free ground ginger

2 teaspoons gluten-free baking powder

½ teaspoon xanthan gum

1 egg, beaten

Preheat the oven to 275°F. Lightly grease a baking sheet with butter.

Beat together the butter and sugar in a bowl, then sift in the dry ingredients. Add half the egg (discard the rest) and whisk together until the mixture is dry and lumpy.

Knead to a dough, then break off a small piece about the size of a cherry and roll it into a ball. Flatten the ball slightly, then place it on the prepared baking sheet. Repeat with the remaining dough, spacing the balls well apart on the sheet.

Bake for 40 minutes until risen, slightly browned, and hard. Transfer to a wire rack to cool.

Ginger Honeycomb Cookies

Lightly spiced and extremely crunchy, these ginger cookies are made using a modified version of a recipe from my mother's friend Rosemary. Their humped shape is a bit unusual, but they are possibly the nicest ginger cookies you'll ever eat. We call them "cave cookies" because the honeycomb texture inside is reminiscent of limestone caverns (children are endlessly fascinated by this and require many samples to fully investigate the phenomenon). You may balk at the amount of sugar, but any reduction and these cookies will go from cavelike to cakelike. They keep for up to 1 week in an airtight container.

⅓ cup whole almonds

2 eggs, separated

½ cup granulated sugar

¾ cup ground almonds

¾ cup Gluten-Free Plain White Flour Blend (see page 164)

pinch of salt

sunflower oil, for greasing

Preheat the oven to 325°F. Place the almonds on a baking sheet and roast for 5 minutes until lightly toasted.

Whisk the egg whites in a thoroughly clean bowl until stiff. Using the same whisk, whisk the egg yolks and sugar in a separate large bowl until pale and frothy. Fold in the ground almonds, flour blend, salt, and egg whites until combined, then fold in the toasted nuts.

Lightly grease the baking sheet with sunflower oil. Using a spatula, spoon the dough into 2 rectangles on the sheet, then pat out to about 3 x 6 inches. Bake for 30 minutes.

Remove the cookie dough from the oven and let cool slightly. Loosen the dough from the baking sheet and cut each piece into diagonal strips using a sharp knife, then spread out the pieces on the sheet.

Reduce the oven temperature to 250°F, return the biscotti to the oven, and bake for 45–60 minutes until pale golden and completely hard. Let cool. Store in an airtight container.

Biscotti

An Italian favorite: try dunking these long, hard almond cookies into coffee, tea, or just cold milk. Add the grated zest of 1 large, unwaxed orange for a citrussy variation on this recipe.

1¼ cups Gluten-Free Plain White Flour Blend (see page 164), plus extra for dusting

⅓ cup granulated sugar

7 tablespoons unsalted butter, softened, plus extra for greasing

grated zest of 2 unwaxed lemons

1 egg

1 teaspoon gluten-free baking powder

½ teaspoon xanthan gum

¼ teaspoon gluten-free ground cinnamon

Place all the ingredients in a bowl and stir together until the mixture forms a very soft, slightly sticky ball of dough. Cover with plastic wrap and chill for 30 minutes to allow the lemon flavor to develop.

Preheat the oven to 325°F. Grease 2 baking sheets with butter.

If you have a cookie press, put in the dough and stamp out cookies onto the prepared baking sheets, spacing them well apart to allow for spreading. Alternatively, turn the dough out onto a counter dusted with flour blend and roll into a sausage about 2 inches in diameter. Slice into circles about ¼ inch thick and place, spaced well apart, on the prepared baking sheets.

Bake for 18–20 minutes until golden. Using a palette knife, transfer the cookies to a wire rack as soon as you take them out of the oven or they will stick to the sheets (pop the sheets back into the oven for a few moments if this starts to happen). Let cool on the wire rack. Store in an airtight container.

Lemon Cookies

If elegance can be ascribed to a cookie then these have it for sure: they're light and crisp with a delicate lemon flavor and a buttery moreishness. You could use a cookie press for a professional-looking finish, but it isn't essential, because they are sure to be popular regardless.

7 tablespoons unsalted butter, plus extra for greasing

½ cup confectioners' sugar

1 cup ground almonds

½ cup plus 2 tablespoons brown rice flour, plus extra for dusting

¼ teaspoon xanthan gum

¼ teaspoon gluten-free baking powder

large pinch of salt

2 teaspoons superfine sugar, for sprinkling

VARIATION

For a nuttier, earthier taste to your shortbread, substitute the ground almonds with ground hazelnuts.

Melt the butter in a saucepan, then add the confectioners' sugar, ground almonds, rice flour, xanthan gum, baking powder, and salt and stir together. Shape the dough into a ball, wrap in plastic wrap, and chill for at least 20 minutes.

Preheat the oven to 300°F. Grease a baking sheet with butter.

Roll out the dough to about ¼ inch thick on a counter dusted with rice flour (if the dough cracks, warm it a little in your hands). Using a 6 inch diameter saucer, cut out 2 large circles, rerolling the trimmings if necessary.

Make a frilly edge on each circle by lightly pressing the flattened tip of a round-bladed knife into the dough all the way around. Cut each circle into quarters, then cut the quarters in half to make 8 triangles. Prick each triangle twice with a fork to decorate. Place on the prepared baking sheet and sprinkle over the superfine sugar.

Bake for 20 minutes, then reduce the oven temperature to 250°F and bake for another 10 minutes until just golden. Let cool on the baking sheet.

The shortbread should be completely hard when cooled (if not, bake a little longer in the oven). Store in an airtight container.

Shortbread Petticoat Tails

This shortbread is rich, buttery, and melt-in-the-mouth, yet also robust enough not to crumble until eaten. This traditional shape is said to mimic the contours of a flouncy underskirt, hence the name. The method used for making this shortbread is somewhat unconventional, but it's the one that works.

MAKES ABOUT 25

6 tablespoons olive oil, plus extra
for greasing

3½ cups gluten-free rolled oats

½ teaspoon salt

¾ cup boiling water

cornstarch, for dusting

Preheat the oven to 350°F. Grease a large baking sheet
with a piece of paper towel dipped in a little olive oil.

Place the oats, oil, and salt in a heatproof bowl, pour in the
measurement boiling water, and stir briskly to form a thick
but not sticky dough. If the dough is sticky, add a few more
oats; if it's too dry, add a drop more boiling water. Leave
until cool enough to handle, then knead to a smooth ball.

Roll out the dough to about ⅛–¼ inch thick on a counter
dusted with cornstarch. Stamp out about 25 circles using
a cookie cutter or cut into squares using a knife. Using a
spatula, transfer the circles to the prepared baking sheet,
spaced close together.

Bake for 25 minutes until pale brown at the edges and there
is no trace of gooeyness in the centers. Transfer to a wire
rack to cool.

VARIATION

It's easy to make different
flavors—add a handful
of sunflower seeds or
2 teaspoons dried
rosemary to the dough
before rolling it out.

Oatcakes

Gluten-free oatcakes are becoming increasingly available,
but often only at a premium. It's much cheaper to make your
own using gluten-free oats (and you'll probably be surprised at
how easy they are to make). These will keep for up to 2 weeks
in an airtight container.

MAKES 6

2 tablespoons sunflower oil, plus extra for greasing

1¾ cups Gluten-Free Plain White Flour Blend (see page 164), plus extra for dusting

½ cup milk

2 tablespoons granulated sugar

4 teaspoons lemon juice

1 egg, beaten

2 teaspoons gluten-free baking powder

½ teaspoon baking soda

Preheat the oven to 350°F. Lightly grease a baking sheet with sunflower oil.

Place 1½ cups of the flour blend in a bowl and set aside. Put the remaining flour blend in a saucepan with the milk, oil, sugar, and lemon juice and heat gently, stirring, until the mixture thickens. Let cool for about 5 minutes, then stir in the egg. Add half the flour in the bowl and stir together.

Add the baking powder and baking soda to the remaining flour in the bowl and mix together. Tip the contents into the pan and quickly knead together thoroughly.

Turn the dough out onto a counter dusted with a little flour blend and gently shape it into a rough rectangle, about 1 inch thick. Cut the rectangle into 6 pieces using a sharp knife, then place the pieces on the prepared baking sheet and dust with a little extra flour blend.

Bake for 15 minutes until golden. Serve warm or cold.

VARIATION
Use soy milk in place of the milk for a dairy-free version of this recipe.

Scones

These airy yet robust scones taste just as you'd expect. Precooking some of the flour blend ensures perfect results. Lemon juice gives added lift, but it also means the baking soda starts working right away so you'll need to bake your scones as soon as you've made the dough. Top with jam and cream for a real treat.

MAKES ABOUT 20

7 tablespoons unsalted butter, diced, plus extra for greasing

¾ cup Gluten-Free Plain White Flour Blend (see page 164), plus extra for dusting

½ cup potato flour

2 teaspoons gluten-free baking powder

½ teaspoon xanthan gum

1⅓ cups grated strong cheddar cheese or other hard cheese

1 egg, beaten

2 tablespoons water

¼ teaspoon cayenne pepper

Preheat the oven to 350°F. Lightly grease 2 baking sheets with butter.

Mix together the flour blend, potato flour, baking powder, and xanthan gum in a bowl. Add the butter and rub in with the fingertips until the mixture resembles bread crumbs.

Setting aside a couple of tablespoons of the grated cheese, stir the remainder into the flour mixture with the egg to form a soft dough.

Roll out the dough to a rectangle about ½ inch thick on a counter dusted with a little flour blend. Trim the edges, then cut into fingers.

Add the measurement water to the bowl that held the beaten egg and swoosh it about a bit to create an egg wash. Brush the tops of the cheese straws with the egg wash, sprinkle over the reserved cheese and a dusting of cayenne pepper.

Bake for 15 minutes until golden. Let cool on a wire rack before serving.

Cheese Straws

Family occasions are never complete without my sister-in-law Hannah making a huge batch of cheese straws using our friend Jane's recipe. I've modified the recipe slightly to make it gluten-free, but it's still flaky and richly cheesy. The straws will keep for a few days in an airtight container.

sunflower oil, for greasing

¾ cup Gluten-Free Plain White Flour Blend (see page 164), plus extra for dusting

½ teaspoon gluten-free baking powder

¼ teaspoon xanthan gum

¼ teaspoon salt, plus extra for sprinkling

1 tablespoon pure vegetable fat

6 tablespoons water

Preheat the oven to 325°F. Lightly grease a baking sheet with sunflower oil.

Place the flour blend, baking powder, xanthan gum, and salt in a bowl and stir together. Add the vegetable fat and rub in with the fingertips until the mixture resembles bread crumbs. Add the measurement water and mix together to form a smooth and very malleable dough, adding a little extra water or flour as necessary.

Roll out the dough to about 1/16 inch thick on a counter dusted with flour blend—the dough should be so thin it is almost translucent. Sprinkle with salt and gently roll over the dough so the salt is pressed in. Stamp out about 20 circles using a 2½ inch pastry cutter.

Transfer the circles to the prepared baking sheet and bake for 30 minutes until very crisp (the crackers won't have browned much, but they will have an excellent "snap"). Transfer to a wire rack to cool. Store in an airtight container.

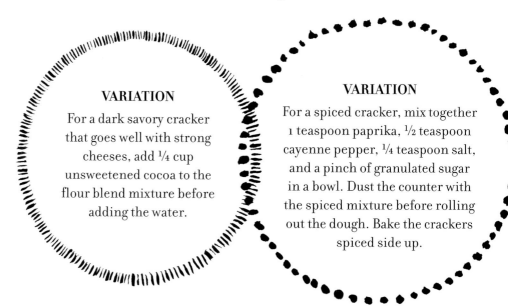

VARIATION

For a dark savory cracker that goes well with strong cheeses, add ¼ cup unsweetened cocoa to the flour blend mixture before adding the water.

VARIATION

For a spiced cracker, mix together 1 teaspoon paprika, ½ teaspoon cayenne pepper, ¼ teaspoon salt, and a pinch of granulated sugar in a bowl. Dust the counter with the spiced mixture before rolling out the dough. Bake the crackers spiced side up.

Crackers

These plain crackers, or water biscuits as they are also known, are lovely to scoop into dips or served topped with cheese or pâté. Try this basic version or go for one of my flavor variations.

4 slices of gluten-free bread

Preheat the oven to 225°F.

Toast the bread on both sides until a light golden brown, then cut off the crusts.

Using a bread knife, cut each piece of toast horizontally into 2 thin sheets, then cut each sheet diagonally to form 2 triangles. Lay the triangles on a baking sheet and bake for 30 minutes until completely dried out.

Melba Toast

Melba toast is a quick and easy way of making crackers if you want something to accompany cheese or pâté, or to serve with soup. The toast will keep for up to a week in an airtight container.

INDULGENCE

vegetable oil, for greasing

1 quantity gluten-free Rich Sweet
Short Pastry Crust dough
(see page 167)

cornstarch, for dusting

2oz milk chocolate,
broken into pieces

18 raspberries

4 strawberries, hulled and
chopped

1 kiwifruit, peeled and cut
into small triangles

9 green grapes, halved

18 blueberries

Crème pâtissière

2 egg yolks

1 tablespoon granulated sugar

4 teaspoons cornstarch

1 teaspoon vanilla extract

1 cup milk

Glaze

¾ cup water

1 tablespoon granulated sugar

2 teaspoons agar flakes

2 ice cubes

Preheat the oven to 350°F. Lightly grease the sections of
2 x 12-cup tart pans with vegetable oil.

Roll out the dough to about ⅛ inch thick on a counter dusted
with cornstarch. Stamp out 18 circles using a fluted pastry cutter
a little larger than the pan sections. Press the dough circles into
the pan sections, then fill each pastry shell with dried beans
or pie weights. Bake for 30 minutes, until crisp and just golden.
Remove the beans and let the tartlets cool on a wire rack.

Melt the chocolate in a heatproof bowl set over a saucepan of
simmering water. Using a pastry brush, carefully spread the
chocolate evenly over each pastry shell, then chill until set.

To make the crème pâtissière, beat together the egg yolks and
sugar in a large bowl. Whisk in the cornstarch and vanilla extract.
Heat the milk until just boiling, then slowly pour it into the egg
mixture, whisking continuously. Pour into the saucepan and heat
gently, whisking continuously until it starts to thicken. Remove
the pan from the heat and let cool, whisking occasionally
to prevent a skin from forming.

When the crème pâtissière is at room temperature, spoon
a heaping teaspoonful into each shell and top with the fruit. Chill
for 30 minutes. Place a saucer in the refrigerator at the same time.

To make the glaze, put the measurement water and sugar into
a saucepan over medium heat. Add the agar flakes and simmer
for about 10 minutes, stirring occasionally, until completely
dissolved. Add an ice cube and stir until it melts. Break up the
second ice cube and add small pieces at a time until the agar
liquid starts to thicken—a teaspoonful dropped onto the chilled
saucer should set almost immediately.

Quickly spoon 1–2 teaspoons of the glaze over the fruit in each
tart. Chill the tarts for 30 minutes before serving.

Glazed Fruit Tartlets

The combination of delicate pastry, crème pâtissière, and
jewel-like fruit appeals to me. Although time-consuming
to make, these sophisticated little tarts are worth it.

1 quantity gluten-free Rich Sweet
Short Pastry Crust dough
(see page 167)

cornstarch, for dusting

2 unwaxed lemons

1 cup confectioners' sugar,
plus extra for dusting

1 cup heavy cream

1 egg, beaten

Preheat the oven to 350°F.

Roll out the dough to about ¼ inch thick on a counter dusted
with cornstarch. Line an 8 inch tart pan with the dough and
trim any excess using a sharp knife. Line the shell with foil
or parchment paper, then fill with dried beans or pie weights.
Bake for 30 minutes until golden. Remove the paper and beans
and let cool.

Meanwhile, make the filling. Cut 4 strips of zest from 1 lemon
using a potato peeler, then squeeze the juice from both lemons.
Place about 125ml (4fl oz) of the juice, the lemon zest, and
confectioners' sugar in a saucepan and heat, stirring, until
boiling. Remove the zest. In a separate pan, heat the cream
until boiling.

Remove the cream from the heat and quickly whisk in the
lemon mixture. Continue whisking for about 1 minute, then let
cool for about 5 minutes. Whisk in the egg. Place the pan over
medium heat and cook, whisking continuously, until the mixture
boils. Remove the pan from the heat and let cool slightly.

When the mixture is the consistency of yogurt, whisk for about
10 seconds, then pour into the pastry shell. Chill for at least
4 hours, or overnight, until set. Dust with a little confectioners'
sugar before serving.

Lemon Tart

This tart is based on the classic French tarte au citron, famous for
its silky smooth, tangy lemon filling. Unlike most recipes, the filling
does not need to be cooked in the oven, but does require at least
4 hours to set. The tart will keep for a couple of days.

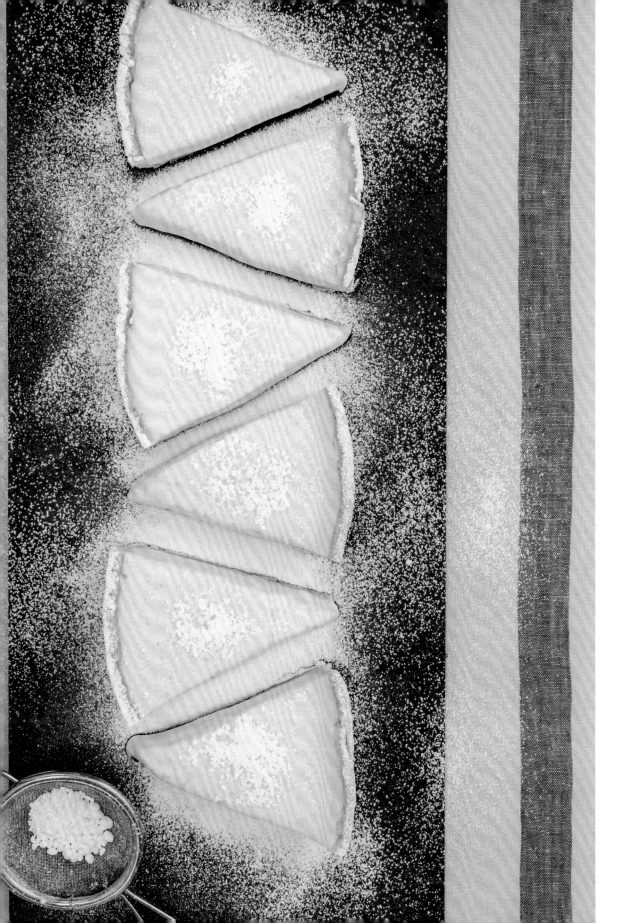

1 quantity gluten-free Rich Sweet
Short Pastry Crust dough
(see page 167)

cornstarch, for dusting

1 cup pecan halves

¾ cup packed dark brown sugar

2 tablespoons maple syrup

7 tablespoons unsalted butter

¼ teaspoon salt

3 eggs

Preheat the oven to 350°F.

Roll out the dough to about ¼ inch thick on a counter dusted
with cornstarch. Line an 8 inch tart pan with the dough and
trim any excess using a sharp knife. Spread the nuts evenly
over the shell.

Place the sugar, syrup, butter, and salt in a saucepan and gently
heat until the mixture forms a caramel. Let bubble for a couple
of minutes, then remove the pan from the heat. Let cool for
about 5 minutes.

Meanwhile, using a fork, beat together the eggs in a large bowl
until just mixed (if you whisk there is a risk of creating foamy
eggs, which don't make for a pleasant end result). Gradually
pour in the cooled caramel, beating continuously with the fork,
then pour into the shell. Bake for 30 minutes until the filling
has set and the pastry is golden.

Pecan Pie

This is a classic tart from the southern USA, packed with pecans
in a toffee-like base. My recipe is less sweet than many others as
I prefer a nutty taste unburdened by tooth-aching sugariness, but
if you like it sweeter, use 1 cup packed dark brown sugar. Pecan
pie is a delicious dessert at any time of year. Try it hot or cold,
with cream.

SERVES 8–10

10oz peeled pumpkin flesh, chopped

1 quantity gluten-free Rich Sweet Short Pastry Crust dough
(see page 167)

cornstarch, for dusting

7 tablespoons unsalted butter, melted

1/3 cup packed dark brown sugar

6 tablespoons plain yogurt

1/4 cup whisky

2 teaspoons cornstarch

1/4 teaspoon gluten-free ground cinnamon

pinch of salt

3 eggs, separated

Preheat the oven to 350°F.

Place the pumpkin in a saucepan, add enough water to cover, and bring to a boil, then cook for 15 minutes until tender.

Meanwhile, roll out the dough to about 1/8 inch thick on a counter dusted with cornstarch. Line a 10 inch loose-bottomed tart pan with the dough and trim any excess using a sharp knife.

Drain the pumpkin, then place in a food processor or blender with the remaining ingredients except the eggs and blend until completely smooth. Add the egg yolks and combine.

Whisk the egg whites in a thoroughly clean large bowl until they form soft peaks. Pour the pumpkin mixture down the side of the bowl, then carefully fold together. Tip the mixture into the prepared pastry shell and bake for about 45 minutes until the pie is puffy and browned. It will collapse a little as it cools, but this is normal.

Pumpkin Pie

This American classic is inspired by an old Pennsylvania Dutch recipe and combines the earthiness of whisky, the toffee flavors of brown sugar, and the slight acidity of yogurt to make an irresistible dessert that will fill your kitchen with mouthwatering aromas. If pumpkin is out of season, butternut squash works just as well. Serve hot or cold, with a little cream or ice cream.

4oz gluten-free sweet
plain hard cookies

1¼ sticks plus 1 tablespoon
unsalted butter

1¼ cups condensed milk

½ cup sour cream
or crème fraîche

3 bananas, sliced

1oz semisweet chocolate, grated

Place the cookies in a sealed plastic food bag and bash with a rolling pin to form crumbs. Alternatively, blitz them in a food processor. Melt 3½ tablespoons of the butter in a small saucepan, then stir in the cookie crumbs until well combined.

Tip the crumbs into a deep 8 inch loose-bottomed tart pan and smooth the mixture level using the back of a metal tablespoon. Chill for at least 1 hour until firm.

To make the toffee, melt the remaining butter in a saucepan over medium heat, then gradually pour in the condensed milk, whisking continuously (condensed milk can burn very easily and if it does you'll end up with dark flecks in your toffee, so keep stirring). Bring the mixture to a boil, then remove the pan from the heat and pour onto the cookie base. Chill for at least 1 hour.

Spread the sour cream or crème fraîche over the toffee layer, then arrange the banana slices over the top. Sprinkle with the grated chocolate and serve.

Banoffee Pie

Banoffee pie is surprisingly simple to make, though it is very indulgent, which is why I offset the sweetness with a sour cream topping. This dessert never fails to delight—provided your guests like bananas. If you suddenly discover you have a banana-hater, then the crunchy base and toffee topping also taste fantastic combined with other fruit, such as blueberries, passion fruits, or—my personal favorite—a couple of crisp grated apples.

3½ tablespoons unsalted butter, plus extra for greasing

5oz semisweet chocolate, broken into pieces

6 eggs, separated

⅓ cup granulated sugar

¾ cup Gluten-Free Plain White Flour Blend (see page 164)

½ cup ground almonds

pinch of salt

Frosting

3½oz semisweet chocolate, broken into pieces

7 tablespoons unsalted butter

1 cup condensed milk

pinch of salt

Preheat the oven to 325°F. Lightly grease 2 x 8 inch sandwich pans with butter.

Place the chocolate and butter in a saucepan over very low heat and heat until the chocolate is almost completely melted, then stir the mixture and remove the pan from the heat. Set aside.

Whisk the egg whites in a thoroughly clean bowl until stiff. Using the same whisk, whisk the egg yolks and sugar in a separate large bowl until pale and thick.

Fold in the flour blend, ground almonds, and salt. Carefully pour the chocolate mixture down the side of the bowl and fold in, then fold in the egg whites until combined.

Pour the cake batter evenly into the prepared pans, then tip the pans from side to side to level the batter. Bake for 20 minutes until a skewer inserted into the centers comes out clean (the cakes won't rise much). Let cool in the pans for a few minutes, then loosen the edges with a palette knife and turn out onto a wire rack. Let cool.

To make the frosting, place all the ingredients in a saucepan and heat gently, stirring, until the mixture is dark and glossy. While still warm, spread a thick layer of frosting over 1 cake. Place the second cake on top, upside down. Spread the remaining frosting over the top and sides. You can make decorative designs in the frosting with a fork, if you wish. Let set for 1 hour before serving.

Chocolate Fudge Cake

This rich chocolate cake is decadence on a plate—dense (but not heavy), moist, and smothered in a thick, glossy chocolate fudge frosting. It is not at all crumbly so it makes the perfect party cake: you can slice it as thin as you like, confident each piece will look perfect. The cake keeps well for a couple of days.

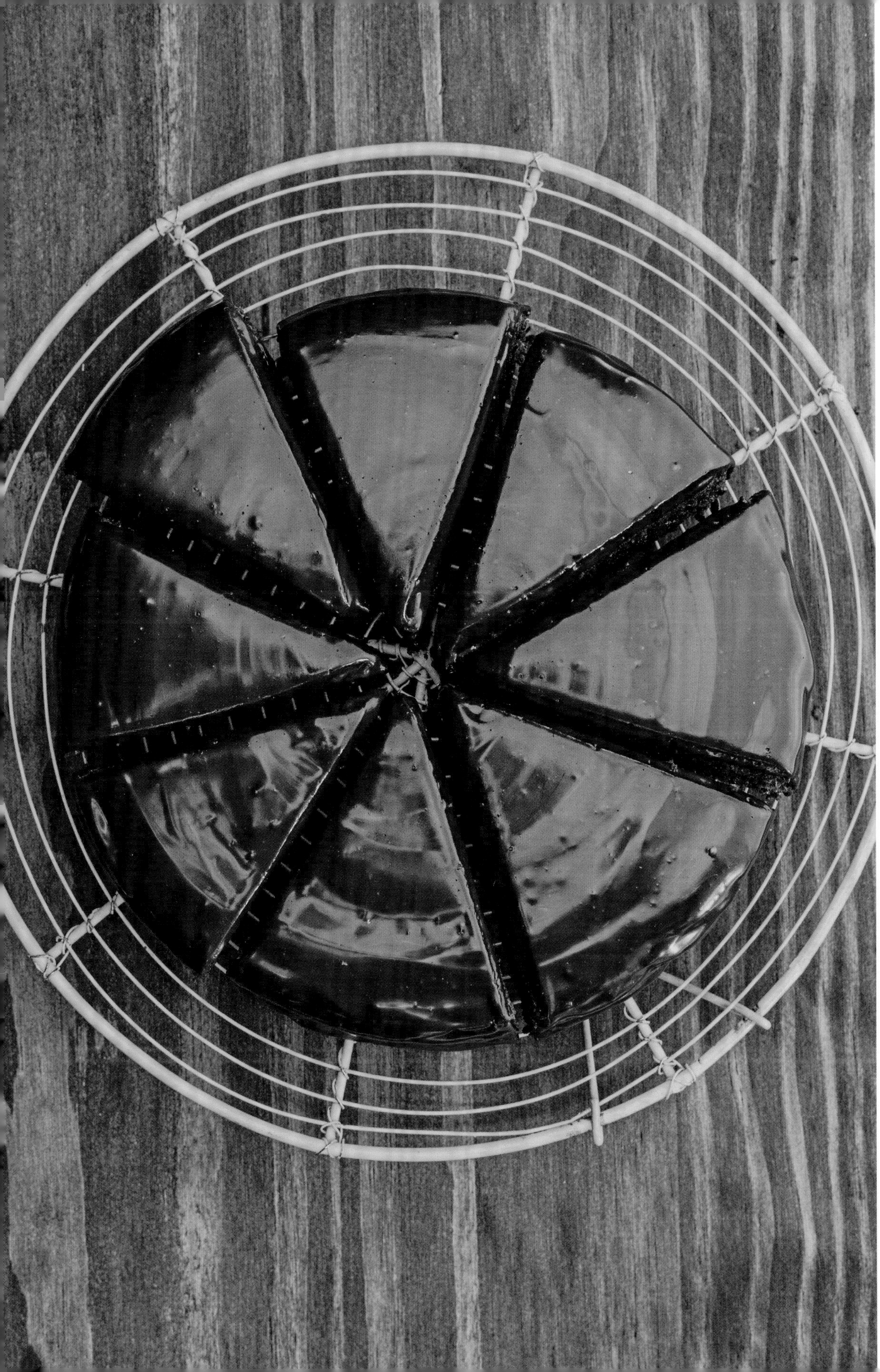

1¼ cups seedless raisins or golden raisins

¼ cup dried apricots, finely chopped

¼ cup black tea

¼ cup orange juice

7 tablespoons unsalted butter, plus extra for greasing

2oz candied cherries, rinsed, dried, and roughly chopped

2 teaspoons gluten-free mixed spice

½ cup packed dark brown sugar

½ cup thick-cut marmalade or apricot jam

3 tablespoons blackstrap molasses

1⅔ cups buckwheat flour

1 cup ground almonds

4 teaspoons gluten-free baking powder

2 eggs, lightly beaten

¼ teaspoon salt

Place the raisins or golden raisins, apricots, tea, and orange juice in a bowl. Let soak overnight.

The next day, preheat the oven to 250°F. Wrap the outside of a deep 8 inch cake pan with a piece of nonstick parchment paper folded lengthwise twice to create a four-layered strip (the extra layers prevent the outside of the cake getting too dry). Grease the inside of the pan with a little butter.

Place the cherries in a small bowl, sprinkle with the mixed spice, and stir together.

Melt the butter in a saucepan, then stir in the sugar, marmalade or jam, and molasses. Add the buckwheat flour, ground almonds, baking powder, eggs, and salt. Stir until well combined, then fold in the spiced cherries and soaked fruit.

Spoon the batter into the prepared pan and level the top. Cover the pan with foil, then prick a few holes in the foil with a skewer. Bake for 3½ hours until well browned—do not open the oven door during the cooking time. A skewer inserted into the center should come out clean. Let cool in the tin.

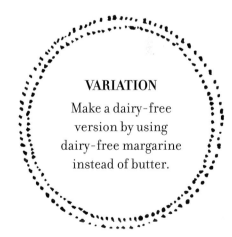

VARIATION
Make a dairy-free version by using dairy-free margarine instead of butter.

Rich Fruit Cake

This is a spiced fruit cake packed with raisins, apricots, and cherries. For best results a little forethought is needed: the fruit should ideally soak overnight and the cake is also better if left for a day or two before it is eaten.

sunflower oil, for greasing

1⅓ cups whole hazelnuts

6 eggs, separated

1⅓ cups confectioners' sugar

Raspberry cream

1½ cups whipping cream

2½ cups fresh raspberries

¼ cup confectioners' sugar

Preheat the oven to 325°F. Lightly grease 2 x 8 inch sandwich pans with sunflower oil and line the bottoms with nonstick parchment paper.

Place the hazelnuts on a baking sheet and roast for 10 minutes. Let cool for 5 minutes, then blitz in a food processor until the texture of coffee grinds.

Whisk the egg whites in a thoroughly clean large bowl until stiff (you should be able to hold the bowl upside down without the whites falling out). Using the same whisk, whisk the confectioners' sugar and egg yolks in a separate bowl until pale and mousse-like. Carefully fold the yolk mixture into the egg whites, then fold in the ground hazelnuts and combine well.

Divide the batter evenly between the pans and bake for 20 minutes until set. Let cool in the pans.

Meanwhile, whip the cream in a large bowl. Using a fork, mash half of the raspberries with the confectioners' sugar in a separate bowl (set aside the best raspberries for decoration), then fold into the cream.

Turn out the cakes onto a wire rack and peel off the parchment paper. Using a bread knife, cut each cake horizontally into 2 even layers.

To assemble, place a layer of cake on a large, flat serving dish and spread over a ½ inch thick layer of the raspberry cream using a spatula. Repeat with the remaining cakes and cream. Decorate with the reserved raspberries and eat on the same day.

Raspberry Hazelnut Gateau

This delicious gateau has voluptuous raspberry-flavored cream billowing across four layers of moist hazelnut sponge. But it's not just pretty—it's also pretty simple to make.

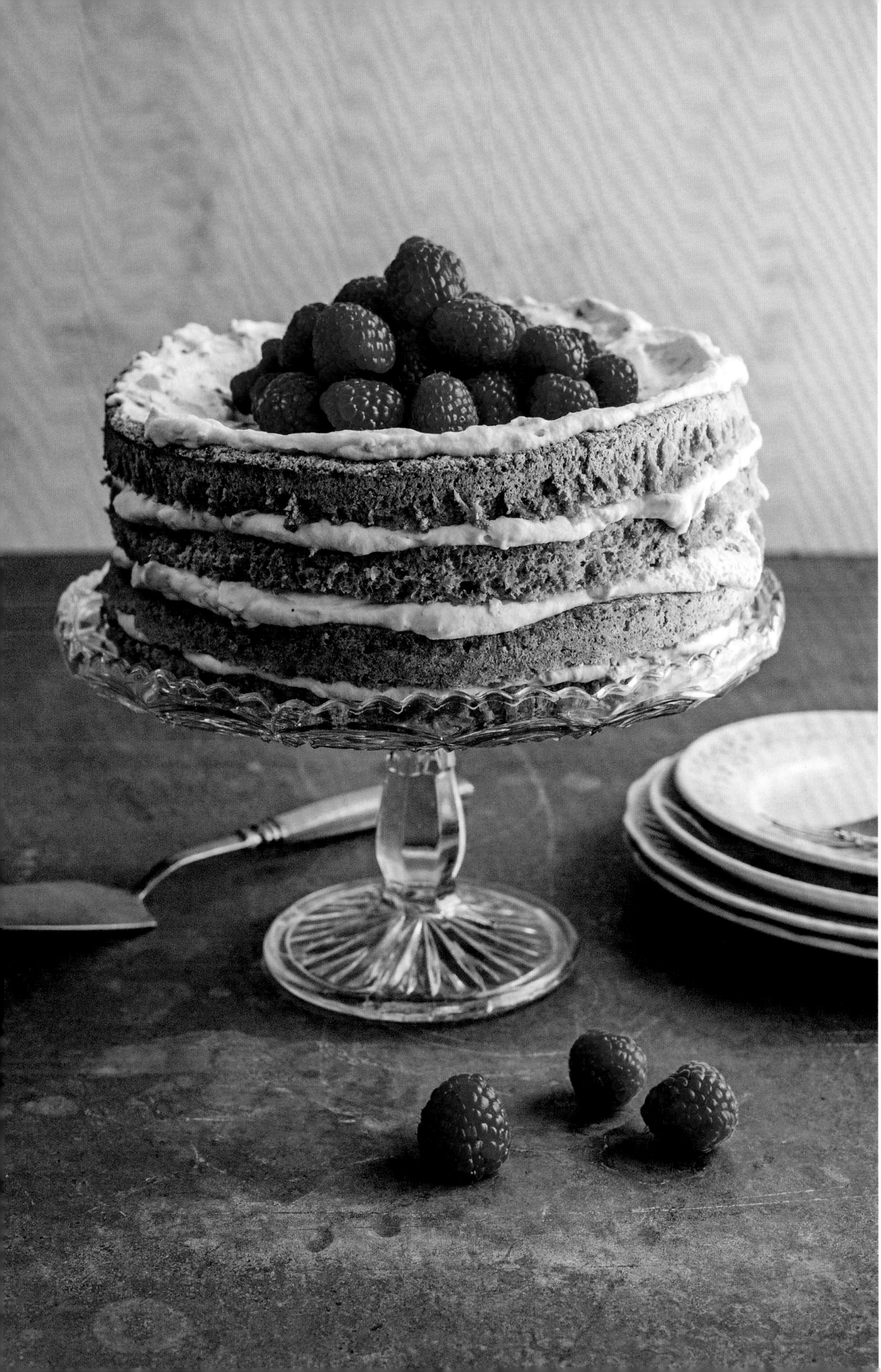

7oz gluten-free amaretti cookies, broken into small pieces

½ cup strong coffee or espresso, cooled

¼ cup brandy

2 eggs, separated

1 tablespoon dark brown sugar

2 teaspoons vanilla extract

1⅓ cups mascarpone

1oz milk chocolate, finely grated, to serve

Place the cookies in a bowl, pour over the coffee and brandy, and let soak for about 10 minutes until softened. Stir occasionally to ensure the cookies have absorbed the liquid.

Whisk the egg whites in a thoroughly clean bowl until they form soft peaks. Using the same whisk, whisk the egg yolks, sugar, and vanilla extract in a separate bowl until frothy and doubled in volume. Add the mascarpone, a little at a time, whisking until well combined. Fold in the egg whites.

Divide the soaked amaretti mixture among dessert glasses or wine glasses (the more decorative, the better), then top with the mascarpone mixture and chill for at least 30 minutes.

To serve, top with the grated chocolate.

Tiramisu

Coffee-soaked amaretti cookies lend an unusual twist to this tiramisu, though it does contain alcohol and raw egg so it's not suitable for everyone. This dessert needs to be eaten the day it is made.

INDULGENCE

sunflower oil, for greasing

2 eggs, separated

¼ cup granulated sugar

¼ cup brown rice flour

Filling

5 sheets of leaf gelatin

½ cup dairy-free
mango smoothie

1 cup whipping cream

½ cup confectioners' sugar

Topping

1 sheet of leaf gelatin

¼ cup dairy-free mango smoothie

2 large passion fruits, seeds
and juice

Preheat the oven to 350°F. Grease the sides of a deep 7 inch springform cake pan with sunflower oil and line the bottom with nonstick parchment paper.

Whisk the egg whites in a clean bowl until they form soft peaks. Whisk the egg yolks and sugar in a separate large bowl until pale and thick. Sift the rice flour into the yolk mixture and fold in with a metal spoon, then fold in the whites, taking care to retain as much air as possible.

Pour the mixture into the prepared cake pan and bake for about 20 minutes until golden. Let cool in the pan.

Meanwhile, to make the filling, soak the gelatin in a bowl of cold water for 5 minutes until soft. Drain, then add to the mango smoothie and heat gently (I do this in a microwave) until the gelatin dissolves. Stir, then let stand for about 20 minutes until it reaches room temperature.

Gently run a knife around the sides of the cake pan, then turn the sponge out onto a large plate. Clean the pan, then lightly grease the sides with sunflower oil. Place the sponge upside down in the pan and carefully remove the parchment paper.

Whip the cream and confectioners' sugar in a bowl until firm, then fold in the gelatin mixture. Pour the mixture into the pan and smooth the top using a spatula. Chill for about 2 hours.

To make the topping, soak the gelatin in cold water for 5 minutes until soft. Drain, then add to the mango smoothie and heat gently until the gelatin dissolves. Let stand for about 20 minutes.

Stir the passion fruit pulp into the gelatin mixture, then pour into the pan, completely covering the fruit cream. Chill for 1 hour. To serve, carefully run a palette knife around the inside of the pan to loosen the cake, then transfer to a serving dish.

Passion Fruit Mousse Cake

Eating this cake is like biting into a tropical cloud. If you want to be really fancy, you can turn the cake into petits fours: use an oiled cookie cutter to punch out as many pieces as you can.

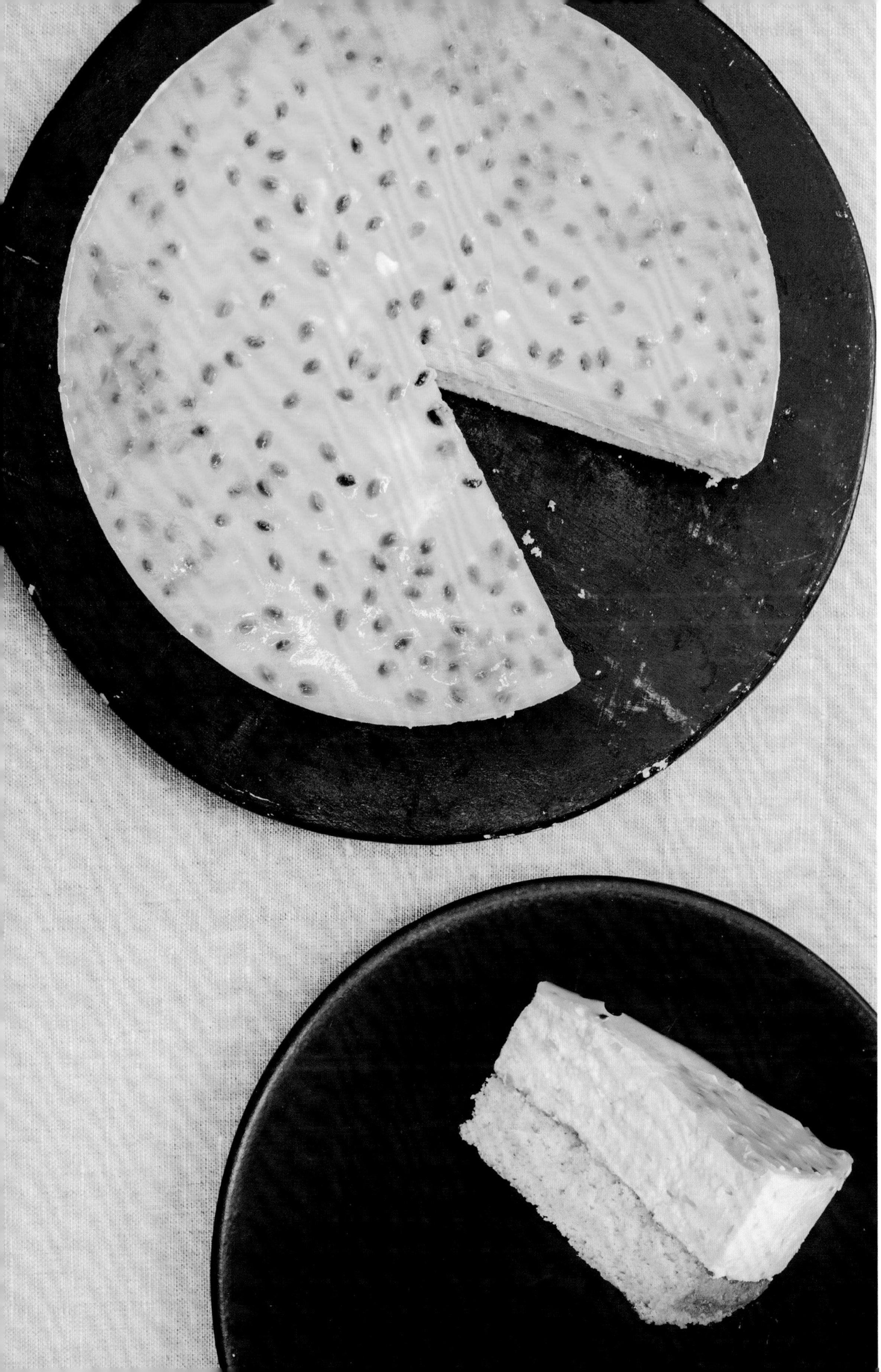

SERVES 6

3 egg whites

½ teaspoon gluten-free
baking powder

¾ cup packed light
brown sugar

⅓ cup slivered almonds

2½ cups gluten-free cornflakes

To serve

1 cup whipping cream

1 kiwifruit, peeled and thinly
sliced

6oz green seedless grapes

Preheat the oven to 325°F. Line an 8 inch tart pan with nonstick parchment paper.

Whisk together the egg whites and baking powder in a thoroughly clean bowl until very stiff (you should be able to hold the bowl upside down without the whites falling out). Gradually whisk in the sugar, a little at a time. Set aside.

Toast the almonds in a small dry skillet over medium-high heat for a few minutes until golden brown, stirring frequently to prevent them burning.

Using a food mixer or mortar and pestle, crush the cornflakes into crumbs. Fold the crumbs and toasted almonds into the meringue mixture.

Pour the mixture into the prepared pan and bake for 40 minutes until puffy and slightly browned (the puffiness will disappear as the meringue cools, but this is normal). Remove from the oven and let cool.

Remove the cooled meringue from the pan and place on a serving plate. Whip the cream until firm, then spread over the meringue base. Arrange the kiwi slices around the edge of the cream, then pile the grapes in the center. Serve immediately.

Almond Meringue

This recipe is adapted from one given to me by my Auntie Maureen, who frequently makes it for her guests (including me!). It's a cross between a pavlova and an almond tart, with the juicy green fruit making the perfect contrast to the sweet nutty, chewy base.

11½oz carrots,
peeled and sliced

2oz dried pitted dates

½ cup light corn syrup

⅓ cup packed dark brown sugar

1 egg

1 cup brown rice flour

1 teaspoon baking soda

¼ teaspoon salt

½ cup cold pure vegetable fat

Sauce

1 cup light cream

7 tablespoons unsalted butter

¼ cup packed dark brown sugar

pinch of salt

Cook the carrots in a saucepan of boiling water until soft. Drain, then place in a food processor with the dates, corn syrup, sugar, and egg and blend until smooth. Add the rice flour, baking soda, salt, and vegetable fat and pulse for 5–10 seconds until the flour is mixed in and the fat is ground into small pieces.

Pour the batter into a 1.5 quart (6¼ cup) ovenproof bowl. Cover the ovenproof bowl with a piece of pleated foil and secure with cook's string or an elastic band.

Place an upturned heatproof saucer in the bottom of a stockpot or large, heavy saucepan. Place the pudding on the saucer, then pour in water until it comes about one-third up the side of the ovenproof bowl. Cover with a lid and bring to a boil, then reduce the heat and simmer for 3½ hours until the pudding is cooked through.

To make the sauce, place all the ingredients in a saucepan and heat gently until the sugar has dissolved, then bring to a boil and cook until thickened.

Run a knife around the edge of the bowl to loosen the pudding, then turn it out onto a plate. Pour over the hot sauce and serve.

If not required immediately, the cooked pudding will keep in the refrigerator for a couple of days. To reheat, cook the pudding as above for 1 hour or remove the foil, loosely place a saucer on top of the bowl, and microwave on medium-high for about 5 minutes until the pudding is piping hot.

Sticky Toffee Pudding

I've drawn on traditional techniques to create this steamed syrup and date sponge—carrots help to create its light texture. The sponge is served with a toffee sauce so heavenly it would make angels weep.

SERVES 6

2 tablespoons unsalted butter, plus extra for greasing

½ cup plus 2 tablespoons brown rice flour

½ cup granulated sugar

½ cup milk

1 teaspoon vanilla extract

½ cup cornstarch

1 tablespoon unsweetened cocoa

2 teaspoons gluten-free baking powder

1 egg, lightly beaten

Sauce

½ cup packed dark brown sugar

¼ cup unsweetened cocoa

1 cup boiling water

¾ cup milk

Preheat the oven to 340°F. Grease a 1½ quart (7½ cup) ovenproof bowl with butter.

Place the rice flour, sugar, butter, milk, and vanilla extract in a saucepan and whisk together over medium-low heat until the butter has melted and the mixture has thickened to form a paste.

Remove the pan from the heat and whisk in the cornstarch, cocoa, baking powder, and egg. Spoon the batter into the prepared ovenproof bowl.

For the sauce, sprinkle the brown sugar and cocoa over the batter, then pour on the measurement boiling water and milk. Place on a baking sheet and bake for 45–50 minutes until risen and the sauce has a custard-like consistency.

Remove from the oven and let cool for 5–10 minutes. Carefully invert onto a lipped plate or shallow bowl and serve immediately.

Hot Chocolate Pudding

A touch of oven magic turns a large dollop of cake batter topped with boiling water into a mouthwatering chocolate sponge with a pool of rich chocolate sauce underneath. Ideally, this dessert should be served as it emerges from the oven, so aim to make it about an hour before you want it. Delicious with cream or ice cream.

sunflower oil, for greasing

3½oz semisweet chocolate, broken into pieces

3½oz milk chocolate, broken into pieces

6 tablespoons water

1 cup whipping cream

Choux pastry

3½ tablespoons unsalted butter

¾ cup water

1 cup cornstarch

2 eggs, beaten

Preheat the oven to 350°F. Lightly oil a baking sheet with sunflower oil. Place it under cold running water to wet the surface, then tip away any excess water.

To make the choux pastry, heat the butter and measurement water in a saucepan until boiling. Remove the pan from the heat and tip the contents into a blender. Add the cornstarch and blend until smooth. Let cool for a few minutes, then add the eggs and blend until the mixture is glossy and thick.

Using a tablespoon, place 12 equal-size dollops, spaced well apart, on the prepared baking sheet. Bake for 10 minutes, then increase the oven temperature to 400°F and cook for another 15–20 minutes until golden brown. Using a skewer, make a small hole in the side of each choux bun to release the steam, then transfer to a wire rack to cool.

To serve, heat the chocolate and measurement water in a saucepan over gentle heat until the chocolate melts. Stir to combine, then remove from the heat. Whip the cream until stiff peaks form. Cut each profiterole in half and spoon in a generous quantity of cream, then sandwich them back together. Arrange the profiteroles in separate bowls or on one large dish, drizzle over the chocolate sauce, and serve.

Profiteroles

Just about everyone loves profiteroles drizzled with chocolate sauce. This gluten-free version is surprisingly easy provided you follow my slightly unorthodox method. The plain pastry buns will keep for a day or two, but the filling and sauce should only be added when the dessert is ready to serve.

SERVES 6

sunflower oil, for greasing

6 eggs, separated

⅔ cup granulated sugar

½ cup unsweetened cocoa

2 (13oz) cans pitted Morello cherries in juice

1 tablespoon rum

1 cup whipping cream

2 teaspoons confectioners' sugar

1oz semisweet chocolate, to decorate

Preheat the oven to 325°F. Grease 2 x 8 inch sandwich pans with sunflower oil and line with nonstick parchment paper.

Whisk the egg whites in a thoroughly clean bowl until they form soft peaks. Using the same whisk, whisk the egg yolks and sugar in a separate large bowl until pale and thick. Sift in the cocoa and fold in, then carefully fold in the whites.

Divide the batter evenly between the prepared pans, smoothing the tops using a palette knife or spatula. Bake for 15–20 minutes until just cooked. Let cool in the pans for about 15 minutes. Run a palette knife around the edge to loosen them, then turn out onto a wire rack and peel off the parchment paper. Let cool completely.

Drain the cherries, setting aside 2 tablespoons of the juice and a handful of whole cherries for decoration. Roughly chop the remaining cherries. Mix together the reserved cherry juice and the rum.

Whip the cream and confectioners' sugar until it forms soft peaks.

Spoon the cherry juice over 1 cake, then neatly spread over one-third of the cream using a palette knife. Top with the chopped cherries, then sandwich together with the remaining cake. Spread the remaining cream over the sides and top of the cake.

To make chocolate curls, run a vegetable peeler down the side of the block of chocolate. Use the curls and whole cherries to decorate the top of the cake.

Chill for at least 30 minutes before serving.

Black Forest Gateau

Real Black Forest gateaux are made with cocoa in place of wheat flour, making them naturally gluten-free. This recipe is adapted from the one by Delia Smith in her *Complete Cookery Course*—it is so tasty that I didn't feel it needed any further messing about. The gateau should be eaten the day it is made.

Base

7 tablespoons unsalted butter, plus extra for greasing

1 cup ground almonds

½ cup plus 2 tablespoons brown rice flour

¼ cup confectioners' sugar

½ teaspoon xanthan gum

large pinch of salt

Caramel

7 tablespoons unsalted butter

½ teaspoon salt

1¼ cups condensed milk

1 teaspoon blackstrap molasses

Topping

4oz milk chocolate, broken into pieces

2 pinches of sea salt

Preheat the oven to 300°F. Lightly grease an 8 inch square loose-bottomed brownie pan with butter.

To make the base, melt the butter in a saucepan, then stir in the remaining ingredients. Using the back of a metal spoon, press the batter into the pan and smooth the surface. Prick all over with a fork and bake for 25 minutes. Let cool in the pan.

To make the caramel, melt the butter in a saucepan over medium heat, add the salt ,and gradually pour in the condensed milk. Increase the heat to medium-high and stir continuously until the mixture starts to boil. Stir briskly for a few minutes until the mixture is thick and golden brown. Remove the pan from the heat and stir in the molasses. Stir well again and immediately pour over the cooled shortbread and smooth out using a spatula. Set aside to cool completely.

Melt the chocolate in a small heatproof bowl set over a pan of simmering water, making sure the bottom of the bowl does not touch the water. Alternatively, melt in a microwave on low heat. Spread the chocolate evenly across the caramel, then sprinkle over the sea salt and let set.

Cut into 16 squares with a sharp knife, then carefully remove from the pan.

Salted Caramel Millionaire's Shortbread

For a real treat, indulge in these chocolate-topped shortbread squares with an irresistible layer of soft and chewy salted caramel in the center.

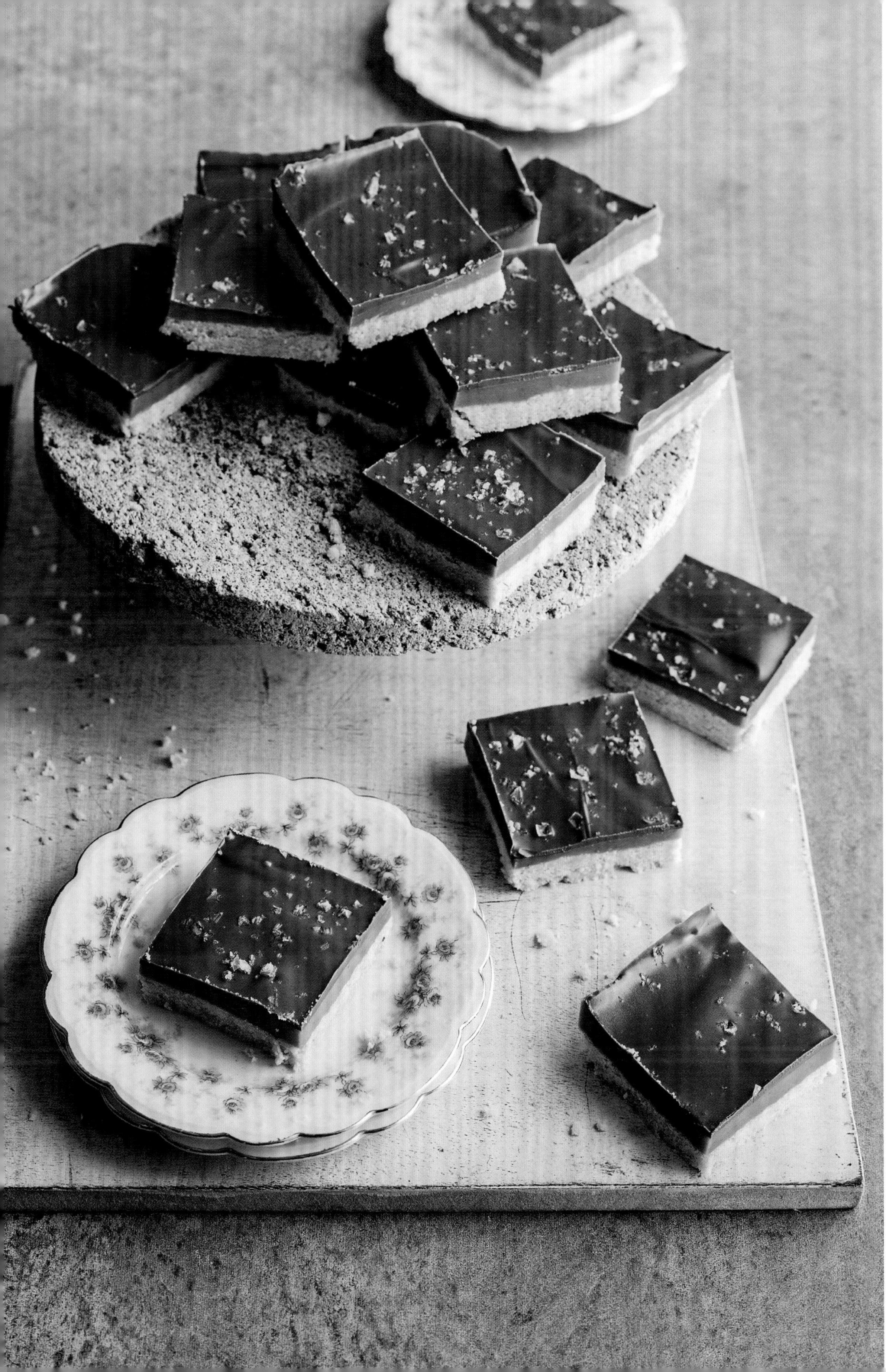

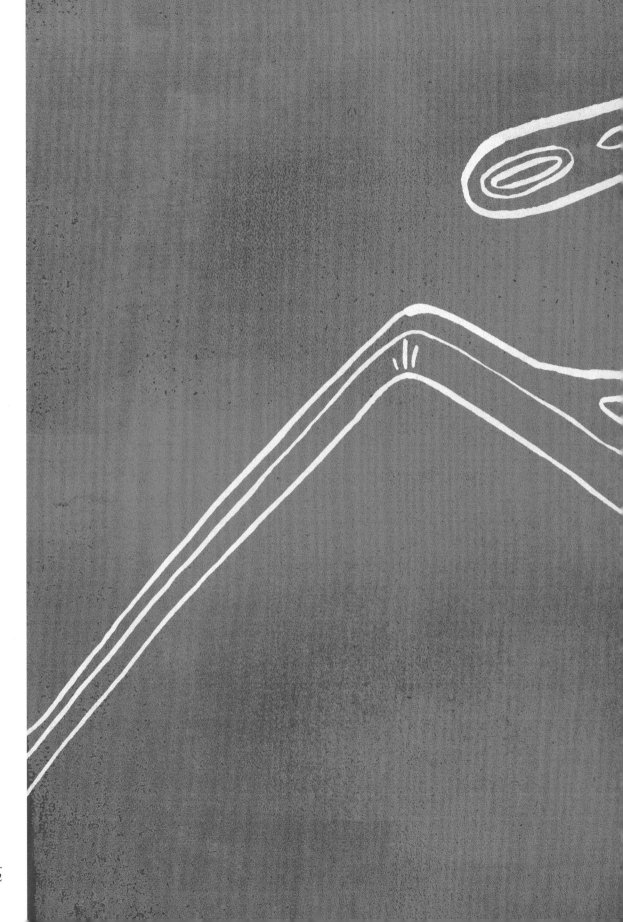

BASICS

2 cups brown rice flour

½ cup tapioca flour

¼ cup potato flour

⅓ cup cornstarch

Place all the flours together in a bowl and stir well.

Sift the flours into a funnel placed in the neck of a storage jar. (This not only minimizes clumps, but also blends the mixture more fully.)

Store the flour blend for up to 1 month, or no longer than the earliest "best before date" of the flours used.

Gluten-Free Plain White Flour Blend

Most grocery stores or health-food stores sell gluten-free plain white flour blends (also known as gluten-free all-purpose flour blends) that are specially formulated to replace white wheat flour. These are usually very good, but if you can't find any or if you would rather make your own, here is my version, which I used for all the applicable recipes in this book. I often make a double batch if I'm doing a lot of baking. I store the flour in a clip-top jar.

¾ cup Flour Blend (see page 164)

⅓ cup potato flour

½ teaspoon xanthan gum

¼ teaspoon gluten-free baking powder

pinch of salt

5 tablespoons cold unsalted butter, diced

¼ cup water

In a food processor, pulse together the flour blend, potato flour, xanthan gum, baking powder, salt, and butter for a few seconds until the mixture resembles bread crumbs. Add the measurement water and blend briefly to form a sticky dough. Leave for a few minutes to absorb the water, then shape into a ball.

Alternatively, mix together the flours, xanthan gum, baking powder, and salt in a bowl, add the butter, and rub in using your fingertips until the mixture resembles bread crumbs. Stir in the water, then knead for 1 minute until well combined—the mixture will seem ridiculously sticky, but gradually the flours will absorb the moisture and you'll be left with a soft dough.

Wrap the dough in plastic wrap and chill for 30 minutes—this makes it easier to roll out.

To blind bake a pastry shell, preheat the oven to 350°F. Roll out the dough to about ¼ inch thick on a counter well dusted with cornstarch. Line an 8 inch tart pan with the dough and trim any excess using a sharp knife. Line the shell with aluminum foil or parchment paper, then fill with pie weights or dried beans. Bake for 30 minutes (or as specified by the recipe) until golden. Remove the paper and weights and let cool.

Plain Short Pastry Crust

This is a very versatile short pastry that doesn't crumble when cooked, tastes great, and can be rolled out very thinly. To be honest, it's even (whisper it) somewhat easier to make and use than standard pastry because there is no need to worry about it getting warm while you handle it and it doesn't shrink nearly so much during baking. It makes enough to line an 8 inch tart pan or make 18 tartlets. You can also make double quantities so you can chill or freeze half for another time. See opposite for rich and sweet variations.

Rich Sweet Short Pastry Crust

¾ cup Gluten-Free Plain White Flour Blend (see page 164)

⅓ cup potato flour

½ teaspoon xanthan gum

¼ teaspoon gluten-free baking powder

1 teaspoon granulated sugar

5 tablespoons cold unsalted butter, cubed

1 egg

In a food processor, pulse together the flour blend, potato flour, xanthan gum, baking powder, sugar, and butter for a few seconds until the mixture resembles bread crumbs. Add the egg and blend briefly to form a sticky dough. Leave for a few minutes to absorb the moisture, then roll into a ball.

If you don't have a food processor, see opposite for an alternative method of making dough—simply use an egg instead of the water.

Wrap the dough in plastic wrap and chill for 30 minutes —this makes it easier to roll out.

Sweet Short Pastry Crust

¾ cup Gluten-Free Plain White Flour Blend (see page 164)

⅓ cup potato flour

½ teaspoon xanthan gum

¼ teaspoon gluten-free baking powder

1 teaspoon granulated sugar

5 tablespoons cold unsalted butter, diced

¼ cup water

In a food processor, pulse together the flour blend, potato flour, xanthan gum, baking powder, sugar, and butter for a few seconds until the mixture resembles bread crumbs. Add the measurement water and blend briefly to form a sticky dough. Leave for a few minutes to absorb the water, then roll into a ball.

If you don't have a food processor, see opposite for an alternative method of making dough.

Wrap the dough in plastic wrap and chill for 30 minutes —this makes it easier to roll out.

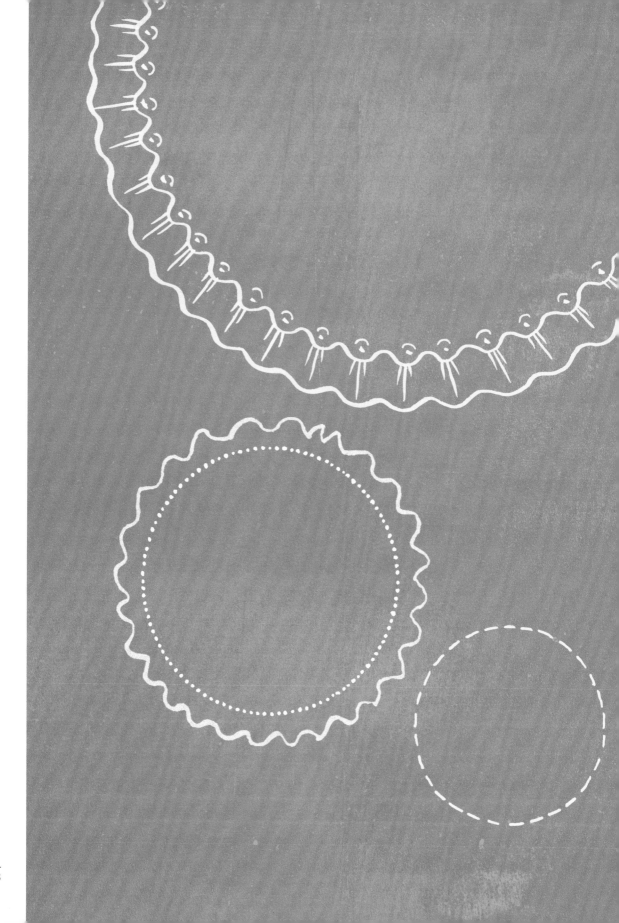

MAKES 1 ¼ CUPS

1 tablespoon sunflower oil

2½ tablespoons cornstarch

1 cup milk

¼ cup gluten-free vegetable stock

1 bay leaf

¼ teaspoon gluten-free
ground nutmeg

Whisk together the oil and cornstarch in a saucepan off the heat. Slowly whisk in the milk and stock until the mixture is lump-free, then add the bay leaf and nutmeg.

Place the pan over medium heat and bring the mixture to a boil, whisking continuously until the sauce is thickened. Remove the bay leaf before using.

Béchamel Sauce

This is a quick and easy white sauce for use in a wide variety of dishes such as lasagna or cauliflower cheese. If you'd like a dairy-free version, use soy milk in place of the milk.

SERVES 4

2 teaspoons olive oil

½ onion, finely diced

1 garlic clove, finely diced

2 (13oz) cans chopped tomatoes

granulated sugar, to taste

2 teaspoons chopped fresh
herbs (optional)

salt and pepper

Heat the oil in a saucepan, add the onion, and cook gently
for 5 minutes until soft and slightly translucent. Add the
garlic and fry for another 1 minute.

Add the tomatoes and simmer, uncovered, for 20 minutes
until thickened. Season with salt and pepper and add sugar
to taste, then stir in the herbs, if using.

Simple Tomato Sauce

This very simple tomato sauce is perfect for serving with gluten-free
pasta or with Swedish Meatballs (see page 82). Try it by itself,
perhaps with a sprinkling of Parmesan, or flavor it by adding
a couple of teaspoons of chopped fresh oregano, thyme, or basil.

1 tablespoon sunflower oil

2½ tablespoons cornstarch

1 cup milk

¼ cup gluten-free vegetable stock

¾ cup grated sharp cheddar cheese

Whisk together the oil and cornstarch in a saucepan off the heat. Slowly whisk in the milk and stock until the mixture is lump-free.

Place the pan over medium heat and bring the mixture to a boil, whisking continuously until the sauce is thickened. Add the cheese and cook, stirring, until the cheese melts. Use straight away.

Cheese Sauce

This rich cheese-flavored sauce is perfect poured over cooked gluten-free macaroni or steamed leeks. You can create a stronger flavor by using Bavarian smoked cheese instead of the cheddar in this recipe.

SERVES 4

1 tablespoon cornstarch

1 tablespoon olive oil

¼ cup light cream

1 tablespoon grated horseradish

1 teaspoon lemon juice

Place the cornstarch and olive oil in a saucepan over medium heat and stir together until well mixed. Add the cream and cook, stirring, until the mixture starts to boil and thicken.

Remove the pan from the heat and stir in the horseradish and lemon juice. Let cool before serving.

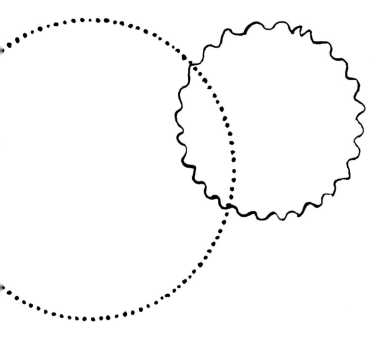

Horseradish Sauce

Some horseradish sauces contain added wheat flour, but luckily making your own is quick and easy. It is possible to buy grated horseradish preserved in vegetable oil, but you may even be able to find a fresh root. This sauce needs to be eaten on the day it is made. Serve with roast beef.

1¼ cups water

1 tablespoon cornstarch

salt and pepper

Pour 1 cup of the measurement water into the roasting pan after you have removed the cooked joint of meat or roasted bird and stir well to loosen all the baked-on bits. Place the roasting pan directly on the stove, or transfer the mixture to a saucepan, and heat through. Strain off the fat. Strain the gravy, if liked, and return to the pan.

Meanwhile, mix together the cornstarch and remaining water in a cup until lump-free. Stir the mixture into the hot gravy and bring to a boil, stirring continuously until thickened. Season to taste with salt and pepper and serve.

Simple Gravy

Although most gravy granules contain wheat flour, you can also use cornstarch to thicken gravy after cooking a joint or bird—here's how.

sunflower oil, for greasing

1 boneless pork chop, about 3oz, fat trimmed and cut into ¼ inch cubes

½ cup milk

2 dessert apples, about 7oz total weight, peeled, cored, and finely chopped

2 teaspoons water

2 (8oz) cans whole chestnuts, drained and crumbled into small pieces

1 small onion, finely diced

1 egg, lightly beaten

2 teaspoons chopped parsley

pinch of salt

Preheat the oven to 350°F. Grease a 35oz (4 cup) pie dish with a little sunflower oil.

Place the pork in a saucepan, add the milk, and simmer for 15 minutes until the meat is cooked through.

Meanwhile, put the apples and measurement water in a separate saucepan and cook over low heat until softened, then drain.

Drain the pork, pouring ¼ cup of the milk into a bowl (discard the rest), then add the pork, cooked apple pieces, and all the remaining ingredients and stir well.

Spoon the mixture into the prepared dish and bake for 40 minutes until browned and crispy.

VARIATION
Make this stuffing dairy-free by substituting the milk with soy milk.

Chestnut & Apple Stuffing

This gluten-free stuffing is a firm favorite in our family where it is always served at Christmas. We almost prefer it to the roast meat it is served with! Although I suggest baking it in a pie dish, you could also use it to stuff a bird or joint.

SERVES 4

1½ cups white basmati or other long-grain rice

3 cups boiling water

Place the rice in a saucepan. Fill the pan with cold water and swoosh it about, then drain out the water. Add the boiling measurement water and cover with a tight-fitting lid.

Put the pan over high heat and bring to a boil—as soon as the water bubbles, reduce the heat to its lowest setting and cook the rice for about 12–15 minutes (depending on the type of rice) until all the liquid has been absorbed.

Fluff up the rice with a fork and serve.

Perfect Rice

If there was one thing my mother drummed into me when I was a child, it was how to cook rice. This method leaves the rice perfectly tender without the need to drain (preserving many of the water-soluble vitamins) and without it becoming overly sticky either. The rule of thumb is 1 part rice to 2 parts boiling water. This makes everyday rice cooking dead easy: just find a receptacle that exactly holds the amount of dry rice you need, then fill it twice with boiling water. Add everything to your pan and away you go.

1¾lb red waxy potatoes, such as
Russet or Chieftain, peeled

1 cup potato flour, plus extra
for dusting

¼ teaspoon gluten-free ground
nutmeg

½ teaspoon salt

1 egg, lightly beaten

Cut the potatoes in half lengthwise, then cut each piece lengthwise into 3. Cook in a saucepan of boiling water for exactly 5 minutes, then drain and let cool completely.

Finely grate the cooled potato into a large bowl. Add the potato flour, nutmeg, salt, and egg, then knead gently to form a soft but not sticky dough, adding a little extra potato flour if necessary.

Cut the dough in half, then each half into quarters. Roll out each piece of dough to a sausage about ¾ inch wide on a counter well dusted with potato flour, then chop into pieces about ¾ inch long. You can leave the gnocchi like this, but if you want yours rounded, shape the pieces in the palm of your hand.

The gnocchi can be cooked immediately. Alternatively, dust with a little extra flour and refrigerate for a couple of days or freeze until needed.

To serve, drop the gnocchi into a saucepan of boiling water and cook for about 3 minutes—they will float when they are cooked through.

Gnocchi

The key to successful gnocchi is the variety of potato—you want a reasonably waxy variety for the best results. Serve with pesto or my Simple Tomato Sauce (see page 170) and a little grated Parmesan.

SERVES 4

1¼lb large potatoes, peeled and cut into ¾ inch pieces

3½ tablespoons unsalted butter

¼ cup potato flour, plus extra for dusting

½ teaspoon salt

Cook the potatoes in a saucepan of boiling water for 15 minutes until completely soft, then drain and return to the pan. Turn the stove off, then return the pan to the ring to allow any moisture in the potatoes to evaporate in the residual heat.

Add the butter and mash with a potato masher until smooth and lump-free. Add the potato flour and salt, then quickly knead into a slightly sticky dough. Cut the dough in half.

Using your hands or a rolling pin, shape each half of dough into a circle about the size of a side plate and ½ inch thick on a counter well dusted with potato flour. Sprinkle both sides with potato flour.

Cook the circles in a dry skillet for about 5 minutes on each side until golden. Cut into quarters and serve hot.

Irish Potato Farls

These traditional, flat Irish potato cakes are almost bread-like when done. They make a great accompaniment to a breakfast of sausages, eggs, and bacon, but they can also be enjoyed buttered and served with soup.

2 tablespoons sunflower oil

1 celeriac, about 1½lb

2 garlic cloves, crushed

½ teaspoon gluten-free ground cinnamon

½ teaspoon cayenne pepper

½ teaspoon dried thyme

¼ teaspoon salt

¼ teaspoon ground black pepper

Preheat the oven to 350°F. Pour the sunflower oil into a lipped baking sheet.

Using a sharp knife, chop away all of the tough outer edges and twisty root parts of the celeriac, leaving just the pithy center. Slice this into ¼ inch fingers.

Mix together the remaining ingredients in a large bowl, then add the celeriac fingers and toss until well coated. Spread the fingers out in the baking sheet and roll them around until coated in the oil. Bake for 20 minutes until browned and cooked through.

VARIATION
You can make plain celeriac fries by coating the celeriac fingers in a little oil and salt before baking.

Jerked Celeriac Fries

While celeriac is undeniably one of the ugliest vegetables around, it does have one major virtue: it's very low in carbohydrates (only about 9 percent) and has various nutritional benefits. Here I've put celeriac to good use by turning it into a few portions of spicy fries.

MAKES ABOUT 12

2¼ cups masa harina

1½ cups water

½ teaspoon salt

Place the masa harina in a large bowl and add the measurement water and salt, then mix together to form a soft, pliable dough.

Heat a large, dry skillet over medium-high heat.

Cut down the sides of a large freezer bag, then take a ball of dough about the size of an egg and place it inside the cut bag. Create a thin, flat dough circle about the size of a side plate by rolling across the bag with a rolling pin (don't make the tortilla too thin or you won't be able to get it out of the bag).

Carefully peel off one side of the plastic bag, place your hand on top of the exposed tortilla, and then flip the bag so the tortilla sits on your outstretched palm. Unpeel the rest of the bag and flip the tortilla into the hot pan.

Cook the tortilla for about 2 minutes on each side until it becomes patchily browned, then transfer to a plate, cover, and keep warm in a low oven while you make and cook the remaining tortillas. Serve immediately.

Corn Tortillas

Traditional Mexican tortillas are made with a specially treated cornmeal, called masa harina. The treatment, known as nixtamalization, was developed thousands of years ago. It breaks down some of the internal structure of the corn and means the resulting flour is more nutritious and can be used in many more ways than standard cornmeal. One common use is in these thin and naturally gluten-free flatbreads. You may need to buy masa harina from a specialist store or online, but it's worth trying, especially if you enjoy Mexican food.

¾ cup Gluten-Free Plain White
Flour Blend (see page 164)

2 eggs, lightly beaten

4 teaspoons sunflower oil

1 cup milk

1 tablespoon granulated sugar

pinch of salt

2 teaspoons gluten-free baking
powder

sunflower oil or butter, for frying

Place the flour blend in a bowl, add the eggs and oil, and stir together. Pour in half the milk and mix together until smooth, then gradually stir in the remaining milk until it forms a thick batter. Let stand for 15 minutes, then stir in the sugar, salt, and baking powder.

Meanwhile, smear the surface of a large skillet with paper towels dipped in oil. Heat the pan over medium-high heat until hot. Spoon dollops of batter into the pan and cook until the surface of the pancakes turns matt, then flip them over and cook for another minute until golden brown. Transfer to a plate and keep warm in a low oven while you cook the remaining batter.

Pancakes

This recipe makes a good basic pancake,
to be dressed up any way you wish: add some blueberries
to the batter, and serve them with bacon and maple syrup.

1¾ cups Gluten-Free Plain White Flour Blend (see page 164)

2¼ cups milk

2 eggs

2 teaspoons sunflower oil, plus extra for greasing if needed

1 teaspoon granulated sugar

½ teaspoon vanilla extract

pinch of salt

Place the flour blend and milk in a saucepan and cook, whisking continuously, until the mixture thickens. (This happens quite quickly and the mixture can become quite stiff, but don't worry about lumps at this stage and just whisk it as thoroughly as you can manage.) Remove the pan from the heat and let cool for about 5 minutes.

Add the remaining ingredients to the mixture then, using a handheld blender or food processor, blend until smooth.

Heat a waffle iron on medium setting. (If it's not nonstick, give it a light oiling before use.) Add a dollop of the batter and close the waffle iron. Cook according to the manufacturer's directions until dark golden brown and cooked through. The waffles are best served hot.

Waffles

Waffles are one of life's simple pleasures —and this method eliminates the grittiness. Try these simply dusted with confectioners' sugar.

¼ cup brown rice flour

1 cup milk

1 cup water

⅓ cup potato flour

pinch of salt

2 eggs, lightly beaten

sunflower oil or butter, for frying

Place the rice flour and milk in a saucepan and heat gently, whisking continuously, until the mixture thickens. Remove the pan from the heat and gradually whisk in the measurement water, then the potato flour and salt. Whisk in the eggs. Pour the batter into a pitcher.

Lightly smear the surface of a large skillet with paper towels dipped in butter or oil. Heat the pan over medium heat, then pour in a dollop of batter and swirl the pan so it forms a thin layer across the bottom of the pan. Cook for 2–3 minutes until golden underneath, then flip it over and cook for another 2–3 minutes until spottily browned. Transfer to a plate and cover with a clean dish towel while you cook the remaining batter. Serve warm.

Crepes

Super-thin yet robust French pancakes are possible with gluten-free flours—you just need to know the right method. These lacy crepes do, however, take a little longer to fry than standard pancakes, so I recommend cooking them in a large skillet. My favorite way to serve these is French-style with a little sugar, or lemon juice and sugar, but my kids would definitely say they prefer chocolate spread …

MAKES ABOUT 30

2½ cups buckwheat flour

2 teaspoons gluten-free baking powder

pinch of salt

2 eggs, lightly beaten

4 teaspoons sunflower oil

1½ cups milk

sunflower oil or butter, for frying

Mix together the flour, baking powder, and salt in a bowl, then stir in the eggs and oil. Gradually add the milk, stirring continuously until it forms a smooth batter.

Smear the surface of a large skillet with paper towels dipped in butter or oil. Heat the pan over medium-high heat. Using a tablespoon, drop 2 or 3 dollops of batter into the pan (make sure they're not touching) and cook for about 1 minute until bubbles form on the surface, then flip them over and cook for another 1 minute or until golden brown. Transfer to a plate and keep warm in a low oven while you cook the remaining batter. Eat the same day.

Blinis

Blinis are savory pancakes from Russia that are often made with buckwheat flour, which has a distinctive taste and is a rich source of minerals and vitamins. Though buckwheat is naturally gluten-free (it's actually the seeds of a plant related to rhubarb), the flour displays similar properties to wheat flour so making these pancakes is straightforward. Serve them hot or cold with sour cream, smoked salmon, lumpfish roe, and chopped chives, or try them topped with egg mayonnaise and a sprinkling of cress.

1/3 cup potato flour

1/3 cup confectioners' sugar

3 tablespoons dark brown sugar

1/2 teaspoon sunflower oil

1/4 teaspoon vanilla extract

1/4 teaspoon xanthan gum

1/4 cup water

Preheat the oven to 325°F.

Mix together the flour, sugars, oil, vanilla extract, and xanthan gum in a bowl. Gradually stir in the measurement water until smooth. Let stand for 10 minutes.

Using a pencil, draw around a 6 inch diameter upturned bowl or side plate on nonstick parchment paper to create 5 circles. Cut the circles out, leaving a border around the edge for you to hold.

Lay the paper circles on a baking sheet. Place a heaping tablespoon of the mixture into the center of each circle, then spread it out evenly to the drawn line using a palette knife. Don't make the edges too thin and don't leave any holes. Bake for about 17 minutes until browned and hardened.

Carefully remove the disks from the oven, then quickly grab the edge of the paper using a dish towel or oven mitt and roll the circle into a cone shape. Hold for a few seconds until the mixture cools enough to be handled; at this point you can peel off the paper and form a tighter cone, pinching the bottom to prevent ice cream dripping out. The cones are delicate, so be careful.

Transfer the cones to a wire rack, seam side down, and leave until completely hardened.

Ice-Cream Cones

These crunchy cones require no special equipment and are just crying out for a dollop of luscious ice cream. The key to success is careful measurement of the ingredients. Store the cones in an airtight container until needed.

GLOSSARY

Here's a quick A–Z of different types of gluten-free flour and other more unusual ingredients you will find in this book.

BROWN RICE FLOUR

Both brown and white rice flours (also known as rice powders) are available. Both are made from ground rice and have a fine consistency. I choose brown rice flour because it contains extra nutrients and has more fiber than white rice flour (which is made from white/polished rice). Not to be confused with rice starch.

BUCKWHEAT FLOUR

Buckwheat is a relative of rhubarb and as such is naturally gluten-free. When buckwheat seeds are ground they produce a pale gray flour with a unique flavor.

CORNSTARCH

An ivory-colored fine flour made from the starchy interior of corn; also known as cornflour. Not to be confused with cornmeal (see below).

CORNMEAL

Cornmeal is also known as maize meal or polenta —a coarse, yellow flour made from corn with the texture of fine bread crumbs.

GLUTEN-FREE OATS

Oats carefully grown and processed to avoid gluten contamination.

GRAM FLOUR

Gram flour is also sold as besan, chickpea flour, chana flour, or garbanzo bean flour. It is made from ground chickpeas and is very high in protein.

GROUND ALMONDS

Ground almonds is the name given to a coarse flour made from pure almonds—it may also be sold as almond meal or almond flour. For the recipes in this book, it doesn't matter whether you choose the kind that includes the skins of the almonds or not.

FLAXSEEDS

Also known as linseed, flaxseeds are the seeds of the flax plant. They may be brown or yellow and are a good source of fiber.

MASA HARINA

Masa harina is the name given to a special pale, fine cornmeal made from nixtamalized corn. Nixtamalization improves the nutritional content of the corn and also means the cornmeal will stick together and form a dough when liquid is added.

POTATO FLOUR

A white starch derived from potatoes, this makes a good thickening agent.

TAPIOCA FLOUR

Tapioca flour is a bright white starch made from the root of the cassava or manioc plant. It is very useful in gluten-free cooking because it goes very stretchy when mixed with liquid and heated.

XANTHAN GUM

Xanthan gum is a sticky substance produced by certain bacteria that is then dried to form a pale gray powder. It can be used for a variety of food-related uses. In gluten-free cooking it is most commonly used to help reduce crumbliness in cakes or pastry, or to provide elasticity to dough. I try not to use it any more than strictly necessary. It is also worth checking the source of the xanthan because the bacteria can be grown on a number of different mediums (for example, wheat or milk) and this may make it unsuitable for individuals highly sensitive to those products.

Index

Acknowledgments

AUTHOR'S ACKNOWLEDGMENTS

Thanks to all those over the years who helped with the various aspects of this book—your feedback was invaluable and I really appreciate the time and effort you spent on my behalf. The list is too long to name everyone, but I'd particularly like to mention the guys in the office (you know who you are!), Allison MacFarlan, Andrea and Gordon Wood, Becky and Steve Boyd, Clare Mills, Felicia Parker, Gillian Randall, Helen Rossiter, Julie Wood, Karin Enskog-Ali, Kim Lankshear, Rose Lewis, Ruth Gillingham, Sanne Williams, Tania Fish, Trish Lorenz, and Zoe Bailey. In particular, I must mention Allyson Bates and Lucie Roberts, my right-hand women!

To Richard, Stanley, Astrid, Torben, Jacky, Hannah, Phil, Mom, and Dad I'd like to say thanks for your patience during my experiments.

Thanks to Eve White and her assistant Jack Ramm for their support and validation. Equally, I am extremely grateful to Fiona Smith for her friendly assistance in the early stages of this process; and Nell Card and Mina Holland at the *Guardian*.

To Stephanie Jackson and all at Octopus Publishing, thank you for working with me on this book. To Alex, Jaz, Kat, Siân, Liz, and Max— it was a pleasure. Thanks to Nina Hertig at Sigmar London for loan of some of the plates.

Finally, to Anne Balme: I am so grateful to you for the many afternoons you spent in my kitchen chatting about gluten-free cooking (not that you had much choice—I talked about little else for months!). This book would never have been the same without you.

ABOUT THE AUTHOR

Susanna Booth is a passionate and inventive self-taught chef who specializes in creating recipes for specific dietary requirements. A former recipe columnist for the *Guardian*, she uses her degree in Polymer Chemistry to offer a fresh perspective on some of our best-loved dishes.

An Hachette UK Company
www.hachette.co.uk
First published in Great Britain in 2015
by Hamlyn, a division of
Octopus Publishing Group Ltd
Carmelite House
50 Victoria Embankment
London EC4Y 0DZ
www.octopusbooksusa.com

Copyright © Octopus Publishing Group Ltd 2015
Text copyright © Susanna Booth 2015

Distributed in the US by
Hachette Book Group
1290 Avenue of the Americas
4th and 5th Floors
New York, NY 10020

Distributed in Canada by
Canadian Manda Group
664 Annette St.
Toronto, Ontario, Canada M6S 2C8

All rights reserved. No part of this work may be reproduced or utilized in any form or by any means, electronic or mechanical, including photocopying, recording or by any information storage and retrieval system, without the prior written permission of the publisher.

Susanna Booth asserts the moral right to be identified as the author of this work.

ISBN 978 0 60063 094 4

A CIP catalogue record for this book is available from the British Library

Printed and bound in China

10 9 8 7 6 5 4 3 2 1

Publishing Director - Stephanie Jackson
Art Director - Jonathan Christie
Design - Jaz Bahra
Senior Editor - Alex Stetter
Ilustrations - Abigail Read
Photography - Haarala Hamilton
Home Economist and Food Stylist - Kat Mead
Nutritionist - Angela Dowden
Production Controller - Meskerem Berhane